50p

(27)

Tropical Fish in the Aquarium

BY J.M. LODEWIJKS, Ph. D.

President of the World Society of Aquarists 1952-1954
President of the Netherlands Society of
Aquariums and Terrariums 1944-1955

ILLUSTRATED BY REIN STUURMAN
AND H. VAN KRUININGEN

BLANDFORD PRESS

LONDON

First published in the English edition 1963

Second edition 1967
Reprinted 1970
Reprinted 1974

© 1963 Blandford Press Ltd.,
167 High Holborn, London WC1V 6PH

Translated from the Dutch publication
Stille Pracht in het Tropische Aquarium

published by N.V. Koek- en Beschuitfabriek
v/h G. Hille & Zn. Zaandam

ISBN 0 7137 0152 8

Printed in Holland by Yselpress, Deventer

Contents

Part 1   Introducing the Tropical Aquarium   5

Descriptions of Tropical Fish and Plants   9

Natural Food   57

Part 2   Species which need special care   59

Descriptions of these Species and Plants   65

Part 3   Contributed by the British Aquarists Study Society

The keeping of an aquarium   113

The health of fishes   119

Index   125

ACKNOWLEDGEMENT

We are grateful to the British Aquarists Study Society for the help
of their Technical Committee in preparing the English edition, and
for their additional notes.

PART ONE

Introducing the tropical aquarium

Life in a zoo can often be animated and lively! But never in an aquarium. I cannot recall ever hearing noisy conversation, nor outbursts of laughter in the surroundings of aquaria, which gives some idea of the tranquilising effect.

There are aquaria in the grottos of South Limburg which might create a depressive atmosphere because everything is subterranean. A similar feeling might be experienced in the beautiful bunker aquarium at Dusseldorf in Germany. But the cheerful building at Charlottenlund, a little north of Copenhagen, which houses large sea-water aquaria filled with artificial coral painted in brilliant colours, induces at the same time an atmosphere of stillness and peace.

The smaller aquaria kept by biological institutes like those of Trondheim in Norway, Roskow in Britanny, or Gloucester Point in Virginia are places where silence always reigns. The same is true of the Oceanographic Institute of Monaco, which attracts more people than are seen at a fair. Even the Marine Studios in Florida, which are visited daily by Americans in their thousands, are always a place of silence and tranquility. This factor may account for the popularity of aquaria and fish-life, particularly in this modern age when people want to escape from noise and turmoil. The quiet of water-life gives them the conditions they are seeking. Sometimes I have asked people why they speak in whispers when they stand before an aquarium. They replied that they did not even realise they did so: only one said: "I think it must be a kind of awe". My personal belief is that a human being is always reduced to quietness and silence when he is transplanted into a sphere of which he is not an integral part. He is acutely sensitive to things which are not a part of his daily round. He begins to think deeply; peaceful contemplation enters his spirit.

It is not surprising, therefore, that many people wish to introduce an aquarium and all that it offers into their homes. Questions are bound to arise about the installation and upkeep of aquaria. It can be said at once there are no great problems as long as we stick to those fishes which do not require special care.

Directions on establishing a home aquarium will be found in this first part, while the second section is on more uncommon fish requiring extra care.

In order to understand fishes, we should realise that we resemble them in many ways. They have bones, which comprise their skeleton and do not differ greatly from ours in quality.

What we call the flesh of a haddock or fillet of plaice are the muscles; the colour is different from that of the flesh of land animals, but tunny fish has the colour of a raw steak. All fish have red blood, the same as we have. On the other hand you will not find red blood in a lobster or a beetle or a garden snail, or a cuttle fish; they have blue blood!—really sky blue, except the beetle, which has blood of varying colour, depending on its last meal. Its blood only serves to transport its digested food from its intestines to all the parts of its body. That is, of course, the function of all blood streams—human and fish.

Our blood, however, has still another function, and that is to carry oxygen from the respiratory organs and to take it to all those parts of the body that work. We all know that work demands energy. A steam engine obtains energy by burning coal or oil. The more air (that is the oxygen from the air) added to the coal the brighter it will burn and the more energy it will produce. But the coal is burnt out more quickly.

When a human muscle, or the muscle of a fish, wants to work, it requires energy from the blood. The heart of a man or of a fish cannot work if there is no food or oxygen, for the heart is also a muscle. Human and land animals have physically to support themselves, but a fish is physically supported by the water just as a balloon or airship is supported by air. Therefore we require more energy for greater effort than a fish, hence more food and more oxygen, and consequently our blood is made warmer through the process.

Food is also necessary to growth. Fishes grow very fast, some are mature at three months. This factor demands adequate food. We have to watch this point carefully, and it must be the right kind of food. Humans cannot live on hay; for we were not made to digest it. Fish should not be given seeds, or products made from them. Therefore no bread or biscuits for our fishes! Fish food must be all manner of live stock from a ditch or pool. In some cases water plants or rotting vegetation are suitable, but it is preferable to give live food. This is available everywhere nowadays in the shape of daphnia.

Oxygen is a gas and about one fifth of the air immediately surrounding the earth is oxygen. When we breathe, oxygen enters our lungs and is then taken

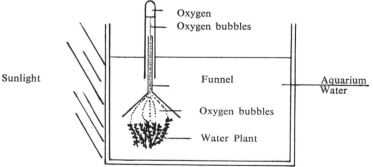

Lighting Cover for the Aquarium

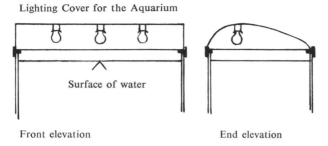

Front elevation   End elevation

up by our blood. Fish require oxygen to be dissolved in the water, but if the water is warm it cannot hold as much oxygen as when it is cold. You can see this for yourself when you fill a glass of cold water from the tap and let it stand in a warm room. Air bubbles will form on the side of the glass. Consequently we have to be careful of warm water in the aquarium. Fishes in garden ponds are sometimes asphyxiated on hot summer days. Tropical fishes can stand heat very much better, for it is natural to them and so they are easier to keep than those in the so-called cold aquarium.

The absorption of oxygen from the water is effected through the gills, which consist of fine layers, and through which the water flows with the continuous movements of the mouth. All these layers together have a large surface and should they stick together as happens when the fish is lying out of the water, then the gills have little or no contact with oxygen; if this continues for any length of time, the fish is suffocated just as men and mammals would suffocate under water, because they cannot obtain oxygen in their natural way.

Like ourselves, fishes have to get rid of the carbon dioxide formed by the burning of food by the oxygen.

Carbon dioxide dissolves in water. Once it is in the water it is not easy to remove it. Water containing this gas has an acid taste. If the water is acid because it contains carbon dioxide, it cannot absorb that which is being given off. If the water is also warm, it can also absorb still less as in the case of oxygen. The fishes try to get rid of the carbon dioxide with their gill movements. Should the aquarium water reach saturation point, especially in warm weather, the fishes will show the same symptoms as human beings who cannot get rid of their carbon dioxide—extreme distress! If we hold our breath a little too long for any reason, we gasp for breath and the heart beats faster and palpitates. Fishes that cannot get rid of their carbon dioxide also have palpitation and tend to swim to the top of the tank. A layman will say: "They are taking a breath of air", and it may even get to that stage. Generally, however, the fish will use only the very topmost layer of the water for breathing purposes, for it knows instinctively that layer contains less carbon dioxide, having lost it partly to the air above the water.

Everyone who wishes to keep an aquarium should be aware of these things, because this excess of carbon dioxide is the cause of death of great numbers of aquarium fishes. Fortunately it is a simple matter to get rid of it. When plants are exposed to the light, the green leaves and stalks absorb the carbon dioxide. This process is essential to their life, and the consequence of their absorption of carbon dioxide makes the plants give off oxygen. Water plants will sometimes give off so much oxygen that the water cannot absorb it quickly enough and little bubbles of oxygen may be observed rising to the surface. This is something we can all observe when the aquarium is placed in the sunlight.

Fishes in an aquarium can therefore only remain healthy if there are healthy plants which receive enough light for them to perform their normal function and keep the water in good condition. The whole A.B.C. of aquarium keeping is to have flourishing water plants. At the same time we have to realise that it is not such a very simple matter to keep plants which come from sun-bathed waters, alive and healthy in stagnant water in a darkish room. During winter there is insufficient daylight for their proper cultivation. So never buy fishes before acquiring an efficient lighting system for the aquarium.

Even lighting does not guarantee success. Plants need food as well as light. The fishes supply the manure and that is amply sufficient. If there should at any time be too much it can be siphoned away with a length of rubber or plastic tubing. This tubing can also be used to take away superfluous food left on the bottom of the tank.

There is a group of very small plants called algae, which do not flower, nor produce seeds, but in the manner of moulds and fungi, they make spores. The air around us is full of these and that air is also carried to the aquarium. Given sufficient light they will grow so quickly on the glass sides that it is impossible to see through them; they will also deposit themselves on the plants, so that these die for lack of light and air. Algae even float in and on the water until this resembles green dye. They are seldom detrimental to the fishes themselves, but they make the aquarium unsightly.

Most species of algae require so much light that they will not thrive with a moderate amount of artificial light, and the exclusion of sunlight. The so-called blue algae feel slimy between the fingers; they are blue green in colour and give a stagnant smell to the water. To remove every tiny piece daily is a good remedy, but needs painstaking care. We shall return to this subject.

Before commencing to instal our aquarium, we at least know that besides the tank itself and water, we shall have to supply living food, healthy plants, light and some rubber tubing. We now also know why. For the time being we shall not buy filters, pumps or thermostats; first we are going to make a success of simple methods.

LEBISTES reticulatus Guppy or Rainbow Fish   Plate 2

Success can be achieved in that same small aquarium with Guppies. The specimens bred here are, on the whole, well able to withstand low temperatures. A room temperature of 50°F or 10°Centigrade is not lethal to them. Yet the Guppy is a tropical fish from the northern part of South America, a territory where frost is absolutely unknown.

It is also a dwarf and belongs to the family of live-bearing Tooth Carps. The males are at least 25 mm. long, and the females below 45 mm. are not fully developed. The males are most gorgeously coloured. All those colours and shapes are hereditary, but it needs much patience and knowledge to develop a stock where all the males are exactly alike.

The breeding is simple; the young just appear in the tank. This is also the case with the *Heterandria formosa,* as both are viviparous, that is to say, contrary to oviparous: females of the live-bearers do not lay eggs, but the young are born and become immediately independent and hunt for food for themselves.

XIPHOPHORUS maculatus with **Egeria densa** (or **Elodea densa**) Platy Fish with Water Plant   Plate 3

XIPHOPHORUS maculatus A red variety of the Platy Fish   Plate 4

The Platy Fish which are found in aquaria in innumerable colour variations are viviparous, too. In Mexico, where they are native, many varieties are to be found, but not the yellow or red types. For all these viviparous fishes, mosquito larvae are the principal, if not the only, food. It may be that the just newly-born will eat very small daphnia. When, for the first time, I inspected carefully very different pools which were the habitat of *Mollienisia, Heterandria* and *Gambusia,* I found great quantities of mosquito larvae, but only a very small number of daphnia. Guppies, and especially their near relations the *Gambusia,* have been sent to all parts of the world to eat the larvae of the mosquito. There seem to be certain varieties of these fishes that eat some algae.

From my observations, dwarf Tooth Carps and Guppies do not appear to eat many green algae, but they do devour rotting algae, perhaps chiefly for the microscopically small animal life and infusoria which certainly live between them. In the pools and streams of Florida, where I found viviparous fishes, there was sometimes a great quantity of rotting plant life, but I could not identify a clear growth of algae.

Platy Fish cannot really be called dwarfs. The males are almost as large as the females and their colouring is not so striking as those of the previous species.

HETERANDRIA formosa
Mosquito Fish   Plate 1

It is always well to start in a small way. Yet that is not the only reason why we commence with this small fish from the most southernly part of the U.S.A.

Its place of natural environment, southern Florida, is not really tropical. The much-advertised luxury bathing resorts of Miami and Palm Beach, with their waving palms, where fabulous sums are asked for hotel accommodation, conjure up visions of the winter holiday haunts of wealthy Americans. But there is another side to the story; an occasional severe night frost will cause enormous damage to the orange-groves and, at the same time if the freezing temperature lasts too long, it will kill thousands of little fishes, although they can stand the cold for a short time.

When fully-grown the males of the Mosquito fish are 11 mm. and the females 26 mm. long, but both may grow larger.

1 *Heterandria formosa*
Mosquito Fish

This is the smallest of the live bearers and it needs neither extra heat, nor a large aquarium. A tank of $10 \times 10 \times 6$ inches will suffice. A 15 watt lamp fixed above it and some planting of *Ceratophyllum* or Hornwort is adequate.

2 *Lebistes reticula*
Guppy or
Rainbow Fish

Adult males are recognisable here, as in the case of the other viviparous types, by their anal fin, which no longer resembles a fin but is a pointed projection, serving to fertilise the female fish.

A tank of $10 \times 6 \times 6$ inches will not be large enough for them: one twice as big, $20 \times 12 \times 12$ inches will be needed. If the little fish are to grow well they must have plenty of room. The temperature of the water should not be allowed to fall below 60°F or 16°Centrigrade, and it will depend on the heating of your room whether this can be maintained. If not, some method must be found to heat the aquarium itself.

It is advisable to buy a good electrical apparatus at the very beginning; a reliable dealer or a member of an aquarium club will be able to advise you.

We may have already noticed that we cannot put all kinds of fishes together in an aquarium. It seems remarkable that it is necessary to point this out; because, in the case of mammals, no one would think of putting a lion and a stoat or an ermine in the same cage, and yet they are all beasts of prey. This, however, is not quite so strange as with fishes, which live in various parts of the world in water of varied temperature and chemical composition. The temperature of the water is, in fact, a matter of great importance. Lion and stoat are both warm-blooded animals, and this means that the surrounding temperature matters little to them. Fishes, on the contrary, are usually just as warm or as cold as the water in which they live. Their organism reacts strongly to intense cold or intense heat. *Heterandria formosa* will still live where *Mollienisia* types have already died from cold. Another type may be able to stand the heat better than the cold. Here, again, other factors play an important part, such as the state of nutrition, the degree of growth, and the percentage of carbon-dioxide in the water. If I say, therefore, that we should not let the temperature rise above 90°F (about 32°C.) this must be considered as a general statement: whilst this rule may not apply to all fishes, it will not be detrimental to them. During warm sunny weather we must therefore switch off the heating.

In Plate No. 3, there is a water plant, *Egerea* or *Elodea densa*, which grows in the southern states of America and is prolific. It is different from the Hornwort, as it develops roots, not so much to take up food, for that is done by the leaves of both plants, but to attach itself to the soil. It is therefore essential that the right soil is provided. As this plant does not take up food by its roots that soil need not contain foodstuff. Therefore, coarse river sand will suffice: it must be washed repeatedly so that when we introduce it into our tank, it does not cloud the water.

Egerea densa is also found in Mexico, where Platy Fish and Swordtail are native. These can, therefore, be kept together in the same tank. Both types are closely related.

11

3 *Xiphophorus maculatus* with
Elodea densa
Platy Fish with Water Plant

4 *Xiphophorus maculatus*
A red variety of the Platy Fish

XIPHOPHORUS helleri Swordtail   Plate 5

XIPHOPHORUS helleri Red Swordtail   Plate 6

Platy Fish and Swordtails need a little extra heat, but they still belong to those fishes that are easy to keep and breed. Beginners especially will be encouraged by the fact that they really and truly have tropical fishes at home, and will be the most likely to give their pets better treatment than those who take everything in their stride. Beginners will often make a great success of freshly acquired or home-bred fish which will develop into well grown specimens.

This can only happen in a largish aquarium, not too densely populated. The male Swordtail really is a splendid fish. He may often be tiresome; he may mistake every fish swimming around for a female of his own species, and he will then start acting in such a provoking way as to become quite insufferable. The female Platy and Swordtail do not seem to object to him. Frequently we can

12

5 *Xiphophorus helleri*
Swordtail

watch the birth of the young Swordtail; an interesting sight for those who have never seen this miracle of nature before. Sometimes the youngsters will drop from their mother and sometimes a little fish will shoot out suddenly head first. It will then tumble slowly to the bottom of the tank. Quite soon after its birth it will start swimming and it will not be long before the little fish sticks, as it were, to the surfacc of the water.

XIPHOPHORUS maculatus with **Acorus pusillus:** Comet Platy (with black stripes along tail fin). Moon Platy (with black spot in front of tail fin). Plate 7

XIPHOPHORUS maculatus Wagtail Platy   Plate 8

An attentive reader may have noticed that a crossing between Swordtail and Platy can occur quite easily. Although both these species are found in the same

6 *Xiphophorus helleri*
Red Swordtail

13

waters, they never cross in their natural surroundings. This is possibly because the behaviour of the males of the two species is so very different that, given a free choice, the female of the species will mate only with one of her own kind. A crossing sometimes causes hereditary characteristics to be upset. The red colour, which on the so-called "Green" Swordtail is not greatly distributed, then permeates the whole skin. I have even seen a stock where the red colour lay like thick blobs on the skin, even covering the eyes. Especially was this so in the case of the males. The black colour in the tail of the Comet Platy runs away in the second generation, so that all the fins turn black, as in the Wagtail.

The black on the flanks of the Platy, as in Plate 3, found in those crossings of the second generation which resemble the Swordtail, causes growths resembling a cancer and this will often prove fatal to the fish rather early in life, but after reaching maturity.

MOLLIENISIA velifera Velifera Mollie   Plate 9

The *Mollienisia* genus has many species such as *velifera, latipinna, sphenops,* etc. The first is found only in Central America; the others are found a little further northward.

Undoubtedly the *velifera* is the most beautiful of them all. I must honestly confess that such a splendid specimen as that shown here is rare. The cause for this may lie in the fact that insufficient care has been given to these fishes. If there is not enough food (in which rotting plants and animal life play an important part) or space (only a few specimens should be kept in a large and well-planted aquarium) the genital organs will develop too early in life and hamper further development.

It is, of course, also possible that the crossing of the various species of *Mollienisias* is another cause, but personally I doubt this. I have myself succeeded in breeding splendid youngsters from bad parents, just by careful treatment and attention to detail. A high summer temperature of 76°F or 28° C. and a low winter temperature of about 60°F or 16°C. give the best results. Then, again, it was more than a year before the difference in sex could be noticed.

MOLLIENISIA species Midnight Mollie   Plate 10

Some of the young which normally have a little black pigment in their skin may develop too much black in their make-up. This curious state of affairs is known as "melanism". This is a handicap to animals in their wild state; they can be more easily seen and therefore, if preying on other animals, they find it more difficult to obtain food. If, on the other hand, other animals prey on them, then they are much easier to catch and devour. But it is different in captivity; there man is apt to search for the exception, and will select animals which lack

14

one or more colours (albinism). Hence albino Swordtail and black *Mollienisia* have a ready sale.

If they are specimens of the true *Mollienisia velifera,* then they will grow to the same size. Their eyes are usually golden coloured. The so-called Black Sailfin have an imposing appearance. The small Midnight Mollies are almost certainly the result of crossings of various *Mollienisia* species. The good ones are intensely black, even their eyes, and they are born black all over, which is not the case with the Sailfin. There are people who, rightly, abominate these creatures as being unnatural. On the other hand, a well-kept aquarium, with bright green plants and filled with blood-red Platy and Midnight Mollies, can look very attractive.

XIPHOPHORUS variatus Platy variatus   Plate 11

That it is very difficult to give aquarium fishes exactly what they require is shown by the species in Plate 11; they are so rarely kept that a really popular name has not yet been found for them. This fish was first imported about 1931. Although it is really very beautiful, it is seldom seen in an average collection. We can only guess why. I know that people who have been extremely successful in breeding Mollienisias and Guppies have been unable to rear the Variatus. These fish have died when quite young. Was there something lacking in the food? Were the temperatures wrong? Who can give us the right answer?

Variatus is only a little larger than the ordinary Platy. The males, when fully-grown, have the most gorgeous colouring. They should be just under three inches in length: they may possibly be a trifle longer—larger than the female of an ordinary Platy. They show a black abdominal spot very early in life. In the case of other viviparous fish like live-bearing Tooth Carps, this spot is visible only on pregnant females, just in front of and above the anal fin. Experts advise that the day and night temperatures should be varied considerably and that the fish should be fed with extra soft fading leaves as, for instance, those of cos lettuce.

BELONESOX belizanus   Plate 12

Amongst all these viviparous Tooth Carps there has suddenly appeared a type which looks very much like a pike and indeed behaves as such. The young if offered for sale, are apt to be very misleading; they can grow to a size of 6 inches, and females have been known to measure more than 8 inches. Fish of this species are carnivorous and can eat up everything alive in the aquarium in one day! Small wonder that they have not become popular, and have not yet received a popular name.

It is strange that one member of the family has developed into a dangerous

15

7 *Xiphophorus maculatus with*
  Acorus pusillus
Comet Platy and Moon Platy

8 *Xiphophorus maculatus*
Wagtail Platy

(Plate 12 cont'd)

cannibal with strong and movable eyes! It leads a lonely life, like every marauder. All the other Tooth Carps live friendly lives in large communities in their tank; in nature, migrating from pool to pool, to rivers and vice versa, according to the season's impulses. They snap at something here, nibble something there, and always have time to jump clear of the water now and

9 *Mollienisia velifera*
Velifera Mollie

10 Midnight Mollie

11 *Xiphophorus variatus*
(Platy variatus)

12 *Belonesox belizanus*

again and stage feigned attacks. *Belonesox,* on the other hand, are motionless, lurking and peering, seeking what they can devour.

Each one in this group in its own particular way gives us interest and food for thought.

VALLISNERIA spiralis Eel grass or Tape grass
ELEOCHARIS acicularis Hair grass   Plate 13

If I suddenly spring a question on someone and ask: "Name a water plant", the answer is most often "A water lily". That is really a mistake. The water lily has leaves which float on the water surface, and are therefore continually in touch with fresh air. If it were entirely under-water it would die in a very short time. Such a plant is of little use in the aquarium, for it takes its carbon dioxide

17

from the air, instead of from the water, and its oxygen is given out to the air, instead of being dissolved in the water. Only the very small seedlings of the water lilies and their kind are useful in the tank. In that stage of development they only have submerged leaves. It is in pools, ditches and brooks that the real water plants may be found. I have already mentioned *Ceratophyllum* or Horn-wort, and *Egerea densa. Fontinalis* or Willow Moss, *Lysimachia*, Moneywort, all found in many varieties, are some of the plants which could be useful in our aquarium, if they did not die off in winter. This is the case with most of the water plants of the temperate zone. For a tropical aquarium it is best to buy good tropical or sub-tropical plants. The various types of *Vallisnerias* can be strongly recommended.

MYRIOPHYLLUM species   Plate 14

Small and giant and twisted *Vallisneria* all have their original habitat in the subtropical areas, as for instance in Lake Garda in Italy, where one type is to be found. There are male and female plants of the species, although the former are rarely found in aquaria. *Vallisneria* has very fine roots; by these the plant can easily be recognised from another plant with ribbon-shaped leaves, the *Sagittaria natans,* a relative of the arrow-head of our ditches. Those roots draw sustenance from the soil, although the leaves take in nourishment. This is even more so with the *Myriophyllum;* they collect all manner of fine dirt, with which the cob-webby leaves will soon be covered. A thickish layer of dirt will finally smother the plant.

   Myriophyllum is found all over the world in every clime, in lakes in a quiet wood or in peaty pools, often with very little light penetrating downwards. With more light they will rise elegantly above the surface of the water, showing by this that they are really land plants.

   From the previous pages, readers will have understood that they should not try to cultivate *Myriophyllum* in an aquarium where restless fishes are kept because by their continual movement they make the dirt swirl up. The same is the case with the plant, a *Naias*, on Plate 15. It attracts all the dirt which may be going.

TANICHTHYS albonubes White Cloud Mountain Minnow   Plate 15

Tanichthys albonubes has a strange history. The Chinese Scout, Tan, discover-ed it (*ichthys* is greek for fish) in the White Cloud Mountains (*albo* white, *nubes* mountains) in 1932. It is a minnow, and is really not a tropical, but a subtropical fish. As it makes little demands on temperature, it is easy to keep and can be bred without difficulty. This is good for a beginner. At a temperature of only 66°F (18°Centigrade) the eggs, which resemble fine sand, are deposited. Then after one or two days, a careful search should be made of the aquarium glass for very thin translucent lines, less than one-fifth of an inch long, and with two black dots for eyes. Those are the new young fishes.

BARBUS conchonius Rosy Barb   Plate 16

The Rosy Barb is not much kept these days. One of the reasons must be that this beautiful little fish is always hunting for food around the bottom of the aquarium, often snaps up dirt, swims with a mouthful of it to the top of the water, and spits it out. Moreover, it is fairly active in its movements, especially during the mating time. This courting causes a continual disturbance of soil, should there be any in the tank. Some plants will fare badly because of this; and so much of the pleasure is taken away. A tank with fishes in it is really beautiful only when the plants also are in prime condition.

But beauty and pleasure can be combined with fishes like the Barb, if the plants do not attract dirt. It is advisable to start with a small aquarium at a fairly low temperature, with easily maintained fishes and plants which make a lot of roots like the *Sagittaria* varieties and the *Echinidorus* types, as shown with the *Puntius ticto* in Plate 25. These roots keep the soil and dirt on the bottom, out of reach of the fishes. Once a good hold has been obtained along the back and sides of the tank, then the water remains clear and more delicate specimen plants can be introduced.

HETERANTHERA zosteraefolia   Plate 17

We must pay due attention to care of the plants. With your garden, if it is not very large, you cannot leave everything to nature, you must prune and prune again, thin out and cut the grass. The smaller the area of garden, the more care has to be taken per square foot. Perhaps you have a lawn in the centre, with borders along the sides, and the tallest plants at the back, forming a foil for the shorter ones in front. Alongside the grass you will have, as it were, cushions of low plants and in the centre of the lawn a single specimen of a well-grown tree, placed so that its contours show up to the best advantage.

I recommend the growing of plants along the back and the sides of the tank until they were well covered. The centre then affords an open space as a restful spot for the onlooker and swimming space for the fishes. In a fairly large aquarium we can try and obtain as a "lone tree" a specimen of the Sword Plant *Echinodorus radicans*. The *Heteranthera zosteraefolia* makes an excellent "cushion" somewhere along the edge of this open space. To achieve this effect, several plants must be set close together. If they grow too high, pinch out the shoots and push them back into the soil in between plants, otherwise they will become willowy and tenuous.

19

13 *Vallisneria spiralis*
  Eel grass or Tape grass
  Eleocharis acicularis
  Hair grass

14 *Myriophyllum* species

BACOPA caroliniana   Plate 18

In another corner, alongside the swimming space, *Bacopa* may be planted. Various kinds can be obtained locally. They need a good light, as do the *Heteranthera*. We should let the *Bacopa* grow a little taller than the *Heteranthera*. It will then have a stately appearance and will always remain upright. We must, however, be sure to prevent its reaching the surface, for it would grow on and on and then the leaves under the water would soon become a thing of the past. This

15 *Tanichthys albonubes*
  White Cloud Mountain Minnow

20

16 *Barbus conchonius*
Rosy Barb

plant has two disadvantages; it may languish and droop on account of algae developing on its leaves, and it demands nourishment from the soil. If these algae are the so-called blue algae (see Introduction), then careful and daily cleaning is the only remedy; if they are ordinary algae, then less light must be given. Food reaches the soil naturally from the urine and faeces of the fishes, but a newly-installed aquarium does not yet possess much of this. Hence a *Bacopa* should not be planted in a newly-installed tank. We shall consider feeding plants later on.

17 *Heteranthera zosteraefolia*

18 *Bacopa caroliniana*

BRACHYDANIO rerio Zebra Danio   Plate 19

BRACHYDANIO nigrofasciatus Spotted Danio   Plate 20

The family name of the two fishes in Plates 19 and 20 is *Brachydanio,* and their outward appearances prove them to be closely related. We know from experience that there may be great differences in a family and that every child, even in the same family, needs its own individual treatment. It is the same in this case. The Zebra Danio, hailing from very shallow waters of India, is probably more used to differences in temperature in its native country than is the Spotted Danio, which is often called the "fourth danio". This name indicates that this is the rarest of the four danio types found in aquaria, not because of its appearance, which assuredly is not less attractive, but because it makes greater demands on its environment. The temperature which, for the *rerio,* may vary between 56°F and 96°F (14° and 34° Centigrade) must vary only very little for the nigrofasciatus; it should never fall below 66°F (18°C) and never rise above 75°F (24°C).

This fish should not be kept in company with others which may snatch food from in front of its mouth; its quick-moving brother *rerio* is apt to do just that.

Only very seldom should the sun be allowed to shine into the aquarium. *Rerio* would *not* object too much, but *nigrofasciatus* would protest in no uncertain manner. The latter needs to play and dart between the roots of plants floating on the surface, such as *Ceratopteris* or *Salvinia* (see Plates 33 and 34), the leaves of which will temper the sunlight.

I watched *rerio* lay their eggs in full sunshine in a little pool in my garden: like the herring, the whole shoal laid at the same time. The widely divergent temperature of that little pool 32 inches deep, basking during the day in the full sunshine of that summer, was soon cooled down in the evening by a sea breeze and the radiation of a clear night. That suited my rerios. In fact, I never saw them so gorgeous; there was a golden glow on the females and a copper glow on the males. They were still alive in that pond after night frosts had caused a little ice to be on the surface of the water. There have been many reports of rerios which furnished healthy young though ice had been in the tank and the eggs had been kept for days at a temperature of only 42°F (5°C).

Let this once more be a warning against making a collection of fishes of all manner of species and families; they should be chosen and grouped according to conditions that suit them.

BRACHYDANIO albolineatus Pearl Danio   Plate 21

Some species of Danios referred to in these pages live not only in stagnant water but also in streams; often so high up in the mountains that night frosts are a possibility. Differences in temperature do not affect them greatly; but muddy surroundings can quickly cause them distress.

All these Danios are delightfully lively. They are fantastic swimmers and are therefore quite difficult to catch in the tank. This is most obvious when at least ten specimens of each variety are kept. They will tumble and race through the water in a gay and unending game. They never pause for long at the bottom, and should they be all together at the top, there is something seriously wrong with your tank.

They do not hide, but are always in the middle layers of the aquarium and therefore attract attention to themselves.

DANIO malabaricus Giant Danio   Plate 22

A small shoal of *Malabaricus* soon gives the impression of a shoal of herring and this largish fish is often described as such. Some may find this species too big for their tank. It would, of course, be more correct to say that the tank was too small for the fish. I like to see them in a tank about 6 feet long, with plenty of swimming space and an extensive planting. All Danios are easy to breed. The only snag is that they eat many eggs; so some method must be devised to prevent this.

One way is to make the fish deposit their eggs in some position in which they cannot readily find them again, such as rough pebbles or a planting of the so-called Hair grass *(Eleocharis acicularis)* which is shown with the *Vallisneria* in Plate 13. The newly-developed young do not resemble the splinters of glass as I described in the case of the *Tanichthys albonubes* in Plate 15, but they are dark. The small fry will eat things so small that they are invisible to the naked eye. Those small organisms are, usually speaking, not present in our aquaria, at least not in sufficient numbers. We can, however, easily catch this food in pools or ponds, preferably in those where ducks are swimming. To attempt to go into more details about this would lead us too far astray. To find out more, the best way is to join a club, where all such matters are easily explained. Standard specialised literature on the subject may also be consulted.

ESOMUS danrica Flying Barb   Plate 23

At first sight these fishes resemble the Danios; as they are related, this is not surprising. The barbels which, especially in the *Brachydanio albolineatus,* are clearly visible, are in this case much longer; there are four of them in two pairs, the first being short and thick and the second long and wispy. The great difference is in the shape of the breast fins. They are quite large here and peculiar in shape with the long first fin ray.

Danios are also barbels. The name Flying Barb does not mean, of course, that they actually take wing and fly. But they swim very quickly; then come up out of the water and float for a while with the aid of their large breast fins.

19 *Brachydanio rerio*
Zebra Danio

20 *Brachydanio nigrofasciatus*
Spotted Danio

21 *Brachydanio albolineatus*
Pearl Danio

(Plate 23 cont'd)

Everyone who has sailed the tropical seas has seen or heard of a large type of fish called Flying Fish which will sometimes "sail" some 500 feet over the surface of the water. Fresh water fishes do this more rarely, for it might happen that such a fish would fly and come down on dry land. Nevertheless, these little fishes can "fly". Care must be taken that they do not fly into the room.

24

22 *Danio malabaricus*
Giant Danio

23 *Esomus danrica*
Flying Barb

24 *Esomus malayensis*
Malayan Flying Barb

ESOMUS malayensis Malayan Flying Barb Plate 24

Naturally, the extra appurtenances grown on these fishes have, like all things in nature, a definite objective. This is quickly apparent when you release a small fly under the covering of your aquarium. There is no more attention given to a Daphnia or a worm. All is centred on the insect. I have myself observed that the fish did not wait for the fly to settle but caught it in mid-air—in flight. Should a larger number than usual of mosquito larvae land in the tank, of which a quantity in due time will become mosquitoes, the Malayan Flying Barbs know what to do with them.

It is advisable to supply such fishes with a sufficient quantity of small flying insects, such as may be found on over-ripe fruit during the summer months. The maggots are seen crawling round and in about ten days they will pupate. Transfer them in that state on to a large floating leaf on the surface of your aquarium. Everything that hatches out is a delicacy which will be greatly appreciated by *Esomus*.

Naturally there are better and more efficient methods of breeding these little fruit flies, but, again, I must refer my readers to more specialised literature.

BARBUS ticto   Plate 25

Both these species of *Barbus* (Plates 25 and 26) live together in shoals in their native waters and will do better in the aquarium if a dozen of them are kept together which, of course, requires a largish tank. Although they do not stir up the soil at the bottom as much as the *Barbus conchonius* (Plate 16) they do the same thing in a smaller way. and will soon turn an aquarium into a muddy pool if kept in very numbers.

Both species are natives of southern Asia, where the *ticto* is to be found spread over a large area, while the Black Ruby seems to be native only in Ceylon and it does not vary much in form and size, though this does occur in *ticto;* however, it is not immutably fixed. If we keep specimens of the *ticto* in similar conditions, but some with the water at a temperature of 77°F (25°C) and others at 59°F (15°C) after the fishes have just laid their eggs, the young of the former (the warmer) will grow no larger than $2\frac{1}{4}$ inches while those from the cooler water will grow to 4 inches.

BARBUS nigrofasciatus Black Ruby or Nigger Barb   Plate 26

There are many differences in colour with this variety, though, here again, everything depends on circumstances. The colour of this *nigrofasciatus* (which means "black striped") is often such that the scientific name is more apt than the popular Black Ruby. This is because unfortunately so many amateurs buy one pair only of each kind, in order to have as much variety as possible in their tank. The Black Ruby only develops the head colouring properly when more males are around; this is due to the attempts of the male, in competition with his fellows, to make himself extra attractive to the ladies of his race. The male shown here is already more beautiful than most seen by many amateurs. But he can become more striking still with the head, cherry red, and the remainder of the body a beautiful jet black. Such a male is then a real jewel, such as is seldom seen in an aquarium. The great thing is that most of the other males develop an equally striking appearance. The females are completely lacking in this finery; indeed, they do not really need this attraction, since the mating initiative emanates entirely from them.

BARBUS semifasciolatus   Plate 27

BARBUS schuberti   Plate 28

Both the fishes in Plates 27 and 28 are really called *Barbus semifasciolatus,* though amateurs often ignore the "semi". The name *"Barbus schuberti"* is, in fact, nonsense. Admittedly there is a constant hereditary distinction, created in captivity, but this ought not to be a reason for giving a different scientific name. This really is not a matter for the layman. A rabbit which is entirely white may have red eyes, but it is still called a rabbit. Yet such an animal is an albino; it lacks all pigment. *"Schuberti"* lacks some of its pigments, but as a compensation the remainder of its colouring is developed to a more intense brightness. This happens frequently: gold fish are the best examples of it, but it also occurs in gold tench, gold carp, golden eels, gold guppies and other fishes. A good name for this is xanthosis.

Personally, I do not admire this gilding very much. Let the pure form be kept in a small aquarium with a quantity of bright green plants, and the background darkened by a rocky surface produced from gold-glinting Norwegian slate. With a little morning sun slanting in from the sides and other fishes playing about or hunting for food along a fairly dark brown bottom, the delicate green and yellow tones of colour on the fairly large scales of this little fish will make an unforgettable impression.

For these species I would prefer not to put *Myriophyllum* in the tank; a close planting of *Vallisneria* and fine *Sagittaria* and especially *Ceratopteris* (Plate 33) with some floating greenery on the surface and not too clear base can make a beautiful composition. This fish can be maintained very easily. The Barbus will eat almost anything. Daphnia, mosquito larvae and other water insects are appreciated, but they are not absolutely necessary. The way in which the fishes will grub along the bottom shows that by nature they eat all sorts of small worms, and we should feed them on these for preference. Tiny pieces of fish or meat which may be a trifle "off", will be readily devoured. They also like fish eggs; a morsel of herring roe rubbed fine is a delicacy. Dead and decomposing leaves will be chewed and then pulled away forcibly from the plant to which they may be attached.

The temperature can vary between 59°F (15°C) and 86°F (30°C).

27

25 *Barbus ticto*

26 *Barbus*
  nigrofasciatus
Black Ruby or
Nigger Barb

27 *Barbus*
  semifasciolatus

28

28 *Barbus schuberti*

29 *Barbus oligolepis*
Chequered Barb

30 *Barbus gelius*
Golden Dwarf Barb

29

BARBUS oligolepis Chequered Barb   Plate 29

The member of the Barbs which I shall now discuss differs from those already referred to, both in outward appearance and in the way of life.

Outwardly the *oligolepis* is like the previous varieties, but decidedly smaller. These fishes are rarely found more than 2 inches long. But there is a vast difference in their habits. The *oligolepis* comes from quite a different area-from Sumatra in Indonesia, where it lives mainly in the mountainous country streams. As with the *ticto* (in Plate 25) the larger fishes will be found living higher up in the mountain rivers and the smaller ones lower down. In aquaria these fishes develop more slowly when the temperature is higher. In their native streams they have, of course, running water, except during the mating season. With running water in a mountain stream there is no dirt on the bottom. Consequently we never, or very seldom, see these fishes turning up the soil; they do not expect any food to be there. For purposes of procreation, however, this fish will turn to a spot where the water does not run, though it may not be actually stagnant. The interesting thing is that when the fish lay their eggs in the humus on the bottom of the aquarium the fry, upon emerging, immediately dig themselves into the soil, and manage to find their food there. It is only when they are able to eat unicellular organisms swimming around that they emerge from the soil, where bacteria have been their main food supply.

BARBUS gelius Golden Dwarf Barb   Plate 30

I have described how the *oligolepis* lays its eggs outside its normal environment. This is even more pronounced in the case of the *gelius*. During the rainy season this fish will move in large shoals to quiet muddy water, which moreover, is often brackish. The movement will sometimes go on for weeks, and hence the fish will be temporarily in water of a very different chemical composition from that to which they have been accustomed. This state of affairs is impossible to provide in our aquarium. Can this be one of the main reasons why we rarely see this beautiful little fish?

Nor does the *gelius* hunt the bottom for food. The few fishes of this variety which I cared for in my own home died after a meal of the little mud-worm Tubifex. This, of course, may have been a coincidence.

An attempt at breeding resulted in the fishes emerging from the eggs and darting into the thickish layer of soil. That was the last I saw of them. Other enthusiasts also seem to experience difficulties with breeding, otherwise we should meet with *gelius* much more frequently.

BARBUS fasciatus Striped Barb   Plate 31

Here is a very different Barb, which, if possible, likes to move in shoals even more than its relations; it is a restless and erratic swimmer, usually occupying the upper layers of the water. But it looks beautiful when the sun shimmers and glimmers in the tank. The glistening of its scales, flashing in the light during its swift darting to and fro, is wonderful to behold. These Barbs seem, however, to be liable to panic suddenly. With a quick start they will all dart off; they will then turn suddenly at the side window of the aquarium and remain motionless for a moment among the plants. Without any perceptible reason they will then suddenly dart away again. I have never been able to spot their leader, nor to discover what was the signal for their moving off again.

Naturally, this frolicsome play can be practised only in a large aquarium. I advise my readers not to keep this little fish in an aquarium less than 3 feet long. It would probably live in a smaller space, but it would lack something. Direct sunlight during the morning hours is essential for these and some other Barbs. Except for these conditions, the Barbs which we have discussed make few demands.

MELANOTAENIA maccullochi Australian Rainbow   Plate 32

This exceptionally beautiful little fish will also adapt itself easily to the aquarium. It is the only Australian in the whole of this book. It is accustomed to the temperature of the West Australian desert, which is high by day with cold nights, but also to the mountain streams of East Australia. This species lives there in shallow water, stagnant or running.

Thus it is able to live in all manner of water in our aquaria and the most varied of temperatures. In addition to these advantages the species is easily induced to breed.

I really believe we make life too easy for it. We take good care that the temperature does not rise too high nor fall too low. This is essential for some fishes, but most certainly not for this variety. *Melanotaenia* as a rule does not bring added lustre with it; the "rainbow" by which name it is often designated sometimes shows only a "matt" appearance in the aquarium; yet it is a jolly romper that will take all food as it comes and will delight in snatching it away from its fellow.

In order to rear young fishes, give them cold nights at 59°F (15°C) and warm day temperatures of at least 86°F (30°C), making the change very gradual. I can promise some astonishing results.

31 *Barbus fasciatus*
Striped Barb

CERATOPTERIS thalictroides Indian Fern   Plate 33

The tightly rolled leaves, like a wound-up watch-spring, immediately reveal the fact that this is one of the ferns. Moreover, it is a fern which is well able to grow in a swamp with its leaves in the open air. Spores will be made, just like ordinary ferns; spores which will be carried away and produce other plants.

Personally, I do not think these leaves are much like the oak leaf, which is the popular name for the plant on the Continent. They are, however, variable in shape. Sometimes the shape will be found to be fixed hereditarily, and in this way I know of three different widths of leaves. Furthermore the shape of the leaf depends very much on where it grows. On the ground the leaves are hard, wide-spread and tenuous; under water they will be found to be very soft, bright green and fairly narrow. When floating on the surface of the water, they are very wide and flat and a little darker than the submerged ones.

All types will develop new plantlets on the edges of their leaves.

32 *Melanotaenia
maccullochi*
Australian Rainbow

32

The Indian Fern will soon form large clumps so long as sufficient light is available. It is apt to turn into a tangled jumble of greenery, and must be cut back regularly. The wide floating leaves take away so much light from the plants growing underneath that some may droop and die. This must also be guarded against in the case of other flowering plants. The same thing can be noticed in our own country pools and ditches.

33 *Ceratopteris thalictroides*
Indian Fern

SALVINIA auriculata   Plate 34

The plant shown in Plate 34 also grows so fast along the surface of the water that it needs frequent thinning out. It is not too obvious that this is also a fern; it is indeed a particular kind; the little hair appendages suspended underneath at first sight look like roots, but they are also leaves.

These and such-like floating plants including the liverwort *Riccia* are very important to the fishes which I shall describe later, especially to those which like to live in rather foul water. A warning must be given that too thick a layer of floating green will choke the plant life underneath.

34 *Salvinia auriculata*

HELOSTOMA temmincki Kissing Gourami   Plate 35

MACROPODUS opercularis Paradise Fish   Plate 36

When the water begins to get polluted, fishes first of all experience difficulty in breathing. As mentioned in the introduction, this means that too much carbon dioxide and too little oxygen are present in the water. In its own way the rotting process resembles breathing.

Certain fishes are so adjusted to bad water that their constitution can stand this process very well. They are able to absorb atmospheric air, just like land animals. For this purpose a special cavity has been developed near their throat; this has a large, moist surface, which acts like a lung. This cavity is called the labyrinth. With some fishes this works so well that, given damp weather, they are able to undertake considerable journeys on dry land, like the well-known Climbing Perch of the Indian Archipelago.

Both the fishes in Plates 35 and 36, belong to the labyrinth species. The Kissing Gouramis are the least attractive. The picture shows their natural colour. In our aquaria we usually meet with an albino form, which has the colour of a little sucking pig; not all the pigment is missing, but certain colouring has just disappeared, without another colouration taking its place, as is the case with the goldfish.

The peculiar lips of this fish, with the fine teeth, serve in the first place to absorb parts of soft plants together with the masses of live bacteria and unicellular animal life hidden among the leaves and stalks. An arrangement along the gill-splits ensures that this very finely divided food does not leave the body immediately by the same way that it came in. This biting towards one another's mouth, shown in the illustration, which looks like kissing, is a form of love-making carried out by many fishes as a preliminary to the actual mating. The polluted water in which these kissing fishes live is often formed through inundation by enormous downpours of rain, when many herbs and plants are literally drowned and rot away.

The fierce sun shining on the freely floating algae (the so-called water flowering) often turns the water entirely green in colour, and that is the time for the procreation of the Kissing fishes. It is not commonly known that eggs also breathe; that is to say they also have to get rid of their carbon dioxide and for that purpose use oxygen. This would not be possible or easy on the bottom between the plants, but immediately after the copulation the eggs rise to the surface of the water and remain there floating.

With the Paradise Fish and the following types this adaptation goes further still.

TRICHOGASTER trichopterus Three Spot Gourami (the third spot being in the eye)   Plate 37

TRICHOGASTER trichopterus Blue Gourami   Plate 38

The pictures of the Gourami types and the Paradise Fish show that these fishes differ but little in their adaptive qualities for living in foul water. The Paradise Fish can, moreover, withstand a certain amount of cold; this is not to be wondered at when we realise that it is found as far north as Korea, where frost is not a rare occurrence. That this fish is also able to maintain itself in aquaria is therefore self-evident. Furthermore, it will eat almost anything; this omnivorous diet is an advantage. There are specimens that do not have this appetite, but they are in the minority.

The *Trichogaster trichopterus* and the Sumatran type, the so-called Blue Gourami, will eat anything but I have never heard or read that these large fishes devour smaller occupants of aquaria. On the Island of Java, where they are called *Ikan sepat,* they are obtainable on the market, dried and salted. Paradise Fishes, now obtainable in many shapes and colours, and *Trichogaster,* can be observed coming to the surface regularly to get air; at the same time they will emit air bubbles. When the water is sufficiently warm and the fishes are grown and strong, the males can be seen taking more air than usual; they let this escape in a series of small bubbles which do not break up immediately on reaching the surface of the water.

A film of slime is laid around the bubbles. The male becomes very aggressive; another male is not tolerated in the same aquarium, and even females and fishes of a different type are attacked. The blowing of bubbles is now restricted to a small area of the aquarium. A large mass of froth, sometimes as big as a soup plate, is formed. The male fish is always near and woe betide another fish if it dares to approach. The attacks can be so savage that, if no shelter is available, there is a real danger of murder.

If a female of the species is in the aquarium and ready to lay her eggs, she will bashfully approach little by little. Then suddenly, as though gathering all her courage, she will swim the last 10 or 12 inches at a faster pace, straight at the male. He does not attack, but raises all his fins. At that moment the Paradise Fish looks particularly striking. The Gouramis, which don black for these occasions, are remarkably imposing.

35 *Helostoma*
temmincki
Kissing Gourami

36 *Macropodus*
opercularis
Paradise Fish

37 *Trichogaster*
trichopterus
Three Spot Gourami

38 *Trichogaster trichopterus*
Blue Gourami

COLISA fasciata Giant Gourami or Striped Gourami   Plate 39

COLISA labiosa Thick-lipped Gourami   Plate 40

The habits of the Paradise Fish and the Gourami are repeated with the *Colisa* types. The difference is that they make the foam (bubble) most for preference between floating plants, such as the *Ceratopteris,* which we have already disussed.

With all these types the females when ready to spawn, will swim straight to the male under the bubble nest. When the female musters courage to force her attentions on the male, she will swim with her abdominal side over his back, and thus pushes him over a trifle. The male twists further and lies on his side and curls himself around the female. The female is now held by the "U" shaped male, hangs upside down in the water and both fishes shudder. Some eggs are seen to leave the female and rise to the surface along the large anal fin of the male, where they are fertilised and they finally come to rest in the bubble nest. This laying of the eggs is repeated several times. The male then recommences blowing his bubbles under the eggs; this has the effect of lifting them

39 *Colisa fasciata*
Giant Gourami or
Striped Gourami

slightly out of the water (which may be fetid) and thus these eggs actually lie in the air, where they have ample oxygen and can get rid of their carbon dioxide.

The male stays near by to guard the eggs for a few days and during that time little fishes appear. The young fry are repeatedly spewed back into the nest by the parent fish. They have a clearly observable drop of oil in their bellies, by means of which they remain afloat. It is only when this oil is used up that they run the risk of perishing but, as a rule, the oil has fed them so well that they have grown strong enough to stay afloat.

Is not all this very wonderful? Is it not also a fascinating study which can absorb our interest? Those long thread-like suspensions underneath the fish are fins, which are also adjusted as feelers. It is also of interest to know that *labiosa* means something to do with lips, for the dark stripes visible on the chin of the fish give the impression of lips.

COLISA lalia Dwarf Gourami   Plate 41

The last of these *Colisa* is the most beautiful, at least so far as the male fish is concerned. He is also the best-tempered. In the case of previous varieties it is advisable after the spawning to remove the female from the aquarium, or at least to afford her ample means of hiding. As a rule this is not necessary with the *lalia.*

An absolute necessity, however, is a close planting with quantities of floating greenery, preferably using such small plants as the *Salvinia* types (Plate 34) or the *Riccia*. The *Colisa lalia* not only makes its nest between the floating greenery, but also deliberately amalgamates it with the bubbles. It is an amusing sight to see this fish moiling and toiling, and so making the plants more and more slimy as they pass through his mouth, until they finally stick together and in this way create a really substantial nest. The difference in sex in this species is very evident; the female lacks nearly all the blue colour and there is not much red either. Moreover, as with all the fishes hitherto discussed, the back dorsal fin of the male is decidedly larger and more pointed. Therefore it is not necessary for the male to become highly coloured during the mating season. In the case of the *labiosa* and the *fasciata,* the male actually grows much darker during the love-making, just as in the case of the *Trichogaster trichopterus.* Experiments have proved that the darker colour helps the female to find the nest.

TRICHOPSIS vittatus Croaking or Purring Gourami   Plate 42

This is also a bubble nest builder, where everything goes on in much the same way as I have hitherto described. The temperature must not be allowed to fall below 85°F (29°C). When this temperature has been reached in the aquarium we immediately hear why this fish received its popular names. Time and again a definite grunt or croak or purr will be emitted from the tank. Can this be a luring, mating call? We cannot be definitely sure, but I, for one, most certainly believe it. It is the serenade of a fish! Often in the case of the birds, the least conspicuous of them is the most wonderful singer. Can it be possible that this is also the case here? You can see for yourself that this fish is neither very beautiful nor conspicuous. The male does not even turn black.

From experiments made all over the world, it has been proved that fishes can hear. A little later we shall be discussing some fishes that can produce sounds.

Usually, but not always, the grunting is accompanied by the bubble-blowing for the nest. In contrast to the previous types I have never seen more than one bubble blown at a time.

BETTA splendens Siamese Fighting Fish   Plate 43, 43a

It is fortunate that there is a large picture of this fish; otherwise I would really not have sufficient space in which to convey to my readers my unbounded admiration for these submerged butterflies. I was only a boy when I stood by and saw the first importation of these veritable jewels unpacked by a man who was one of the founders of the Club of Aquarium-keepers at The Hague. This enthusiast was as delighted as a child. Something of his joy was passed on to all of us who stood around him.

The females of the *Betta splendens* resemble the males in their natural form. It is quite true that the male will not tolerate another male near him during the mating season—and it nearly always is the mating season.

In their natural surroundings, the male with the greatest show of superiority will drive the other males into retreat. Flight in an aquarium is well-nigh impossible and things may be bad for the fugitive.

In Thailand it is a sport among the natives to let these fishes fight; large sums are staked on the favourites.

With these fishes the procedure of mating is peculiar. The female which, in the case of the varieties previously described, swims with her abdominal side over and against the back of the male, in this case swims with her head facing the abdominal side of the male. By this he hangs upside down in the water, in exactly the opposite way to the former species. In turning over, the female is now upside down, but the large fins of the male are underneath her instead of above. The eggs in this case are heavier than water and will sink. They are then taken from the bottom in the mouth by both male and female and spewed into the nest, where they develop as other labyrinth fishes.

40 *Colisa labiosa*
Thick-lipped Gourami

41 *Colisa lalia*
Dwarf Gourami

42 *Trichopsis vittatus*
Croaking or Purring
Gourami

43a *Betta splendens*
Siamese Fighting Fish

BETTA picta   Plate 44

This relation of the Siamese Fighting Fish, the *Betta picta,* solves the problem in a more elegant way. The eggs, which in this case are also heavier than water, are laid on the bottom. Then the female picks them up in her mouth and spits them in the direction of the male's mouth, which is ready to receive them. He keeps them there until the little fishes emerge from the eggs. By his breathing movements the eggs are kept continually in running water and thus get enough oxygen.

The father fish eats nothing during this time. It lasts, however, only for two days. The picture shows the male with the eggs in his mouth.

TRICHOGASTER leeri Pearl Leeri or Lace Gourami   Plate 45

We conclude the series of the labyrinth fishes with this beautiful specimen of the family, which does indeed become fairly large. It will, however, in most circumstances conduct itself in such exemplary fashion that we can keep it without any difficulty with all manner of smaller fishes.

The movements of these princely specimens are never hurried. If there are in the tank no fishes that nibble fins, the male will grow a beautiful pointed dorsal fin, while the anal fin will develop thready growths about half-an-inch long. When to this is added the glistening skin with the vermilion red throat, if ever one should speak of hushed splendour it must be in this instance.

But we shall suddenly be startled by hearing a hard rap from the tank. We may take a quick look to see if a window has burst. With any luck we shall discover that these fishes themselves make this startling noise. At the same time as the rap is heard, we shall see a large bubble emerging from the mouth. Both sexes indulge in this strange performance.

What is its meaning? Frankly, I have not the slightest idea. Neither the conduct of the fish itself, nor of any kindred fish in the same aquarium, is altered in the least by this exhibition.

PTEROPHYLLUM scalare Angel Fish   Plate 46

It is rather strange to pass from the bubble producers to the Angel Fish. Here, we find stately distinguished movements. It is not, however, the dignity of a prince, but rather the elusive mien of the marauder. Small fishes are in danger when the Angel Fish is around.

This variety, too, can make a noise. Sometimes a rhythmic knocking will be heard coming from an aquarium of Angel Fishes. Then one of them can be seen making chopping movements with its head, while it purposefully swims around another Angel Fish. Only the male acts in this fashion. Evidently he has something to say. Whether the noise has some hidden meaning I am at a loss to explain. It is such a pity that we seldom meet with fully-grown Angel Fishes. They need a large aquarium all to themselves, constant temperature of 79°F (26°C), and frequent and regular feeding during their adolescence. In winter the temperature should be lowered to 68°F (20°C). There are specimens on sale at present which are black at the back; they come from Ghent. And now even totally black fishes are to be found, as well as long-finned specimens.

BADIS badis   Plate 47

These fishes which are so easily kept and which are illustrated in the Plate No. 47, need no more care than those already described. Hitherto we have paid no particular attention to the chemical composition of the water nor to the soil. The temperature only needs a little more attention in certain instances, as I have already mentioned. The rearing to maturity of half-grown fishes has not demanded special food and even the breeding has been generally fairly simple. For the amateur who is just starting, the group which immediately follows still comes within this category.

This small attractive fish with the blue gloss over the fins is another example of a little fish that makes few demands, is easily bred and yet charms by shape, behaviour and, above all, by colour. It is sometimes like a chameleon, at first almost plain grey, then reddish with black stripes, and then suddenly all black. But before that happens the fish must be able to make a small hollow at the bottom under a stone. The male cleans this out and then invites the female to lay her eggs. These stick to everything around, even to the ceiling of the nest. Then the lady vanishes and leaves the rearing and education of her off-spring to the father.

HEMIHAPLOCHROMIS multicolor Egyptian Mouth-breeder   Plate 48

Mouth-breeders do not impress one by their beautiful appearance or their colour. It is, however, their behaviour in procreation which makes them so captivating. The female lays her eggs during a vigorous turning round and round, just a few at a time which are milted by the male. Then she takes them in her mouth. More and more eggs are laid, so that the mother sometimes has some hundreds in her mouth at once. She keeps on swimming with all of them safe there. With this species it is the female that carries out this procedure, and not the male, as in the case of the *Betta picta* (Plate 44). And it lasts for more than two days; it actually takes at least ten days before these eggs are hatched and a fortnight before the young are released. Only then will the little mother eat again. She will often chew a large mouthful of food and feed it to the small fry. After a few moments we can see the little ones taking refuge in the mother's

43 *Betta splendens*
Siamese Fighting
Fish

44 *Betta picta*

45 *Trichogaster leeri*
Pearl Leeri or
Lace Gourami

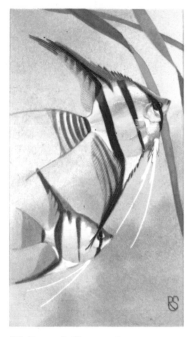

46 *Pterophyllum scalare*
Angel Fish

48 *Badis badis*

(Plate 47 cont'd)

mouth again. It is interesting to know that this process can be watched.

This fish likes to scrabble around at the bottom of the tank, hunting for food; it will then rise to the surface with a mouthful of mud and there spit out what it does not want. Make sure that there is no fine-leaved greenery in the aquarium.

47 *Hemihaplochromis multicolor*
Egyptian
Mouth-breeder

CORYDORAS paleatus   Plate 49

Corydoras belongs to the same Sub-order as the *Ameiurus*, which the Americans call "Cat-fish". *Corydoras*, unlike its relation, does not devour other fishes, but it is something of a glutton. If we wish to obtain full pleasure from our hobby we shall, if we keep *Corydoras*, find it necessary to clean up a great deal ourselves. The excreta will have to be removed from the bottom of the tank by siphoning it away with rubber tubing, otherwise the *Corydoras* will flounce everything through the aquarium and the dirt will settle on the aquatic plants. Some call this variety "the vacuum cleaner"; that may be a suitable name, but the "cleaner" lacks the "bag" in which the dirt is collected. If we are willing to take the trouble, however, these are really amusing fishes, and they will live long. There is one authenticated case of a nineteen-year-old.

JORDANELLA floridae Flag Fish   Plate 50

How is it that we so very seldom see this pretty little fish? Possibly because so many people do not know that this is not a tropical species. The name speaks for itself. It lives in Florida, which state is not tropical but sub-tropical, as I have already stated in the case of Plate 1. Often, without thinking, this fish is kept at 77°F (25°C) instead of at 68°F (20°C).

Though it can stand quite high temperatures for some months of the year, if reproduction of the species is desired, the normal temperature must be kept at 59°F (15°C) or even less. Then, when the temperature is raised, the males become suffused with a reddish glimmer and the females with a greenish gloss. The reflecting scales show up beautifully and at a temperature of 77°F (25°C) the eggs are laid. These eggs are fairly large and stick to the leaves of the plants. The parents do not eat them and the young, which hatch after a week, are left in peace by the parents. The nests are not large—fifty in a clutch is considered to be quite satisfactory.

APHYOCHARAX rubripinnis Bloodfin   Plate 51

Both the fishes in Plates 51 and 52 are small characins. They nearly always have a tiny fin behind the dorsal fin, in which no fin rays are visible. Salmon and trout have this same distinctive characteristic, but we cannot keep them in our aquaria. One is a marine fish which turns to fresh water only for procreative purposes, and the trout needs so much oxygen in the water that it is impossible to obtain enough in our houses during the summer.

Many characins have something peculiar about them and can only be kept alive by really experienced fish keepers. Especially with breeding do some of these apparently insurmountable difficulties arise.

Although the Bloodfin and the Flame Terra are certainly not rare, and are bred regularly, both have the peculiar characteristic that they they are greatly influenced by temperature. Once we have discovered this we can get them to look as beautiful as in the picture.

The Bloodfin comes from clear streams with sunshine pouring down on it; because of the current there is no dirt at the bottom of the stream, and it is clear. In the Bloodfin's original home the temperature is 59°F-68°F. (15°-20° Centigrade); most aquarium keepers keep the temperatures of their tanks at 74°F (23°C). This is too high for this fish and that is why it often looks distressed and unwell. The red disappears from the fins entirely. Therefore it must be kept cool and supplied with clear water on a very clear base.

HYPHESSOBRYCON flammeus Flame Tetra   Plate 52

The Flame Tetra comes from water which has a slack current or no flow at all. All rotting parts of plant life just lie where they have fallen and give a dark hue to the muddy bottom. The water is not even clear, but yellow or brownish. Not many · plants will grow in such an environment, but *Myriophyllum* flourish rather well. The temperature should be slightly higher than in the case of the Bloodfin. It should not drop below 65°F (18°C) but, on the other hand, it should rarely rise above 75°F (24°C).

If kept in light surroundings, over a clear bottom with a temperature below 65°F (18°C) or above 77°F (25°C) all the red is apt to vanish and the fish then becomes a very poor looking specimen.

Even so these fishes are evidently very adaptable or they would be unable to survive in the tanks of many fanciers.

METYNNIS roosevelti   Plate 53

Some years ago this beautiful and somewhat larger species of characin was met with in many aquaria. It is not seen so frequently today and the reason it has not remained populair is that it was found to be a voracious plant-eater.

It is again a species of characin with a peculiarity. I have had one myself for a considerable time and I remember there was one plant it would not touch—the Naias. I admit that I did not give it much choice by offering valuable plants. The fish did very well in a tank with extremely dark rocks here and there heavily covered by algae, and it looked striking by contrast. It ate spinach, lettuce leaves and nettles, but I did not see it devour many algae.

49 *Corydoras paleatus*

50 *Jordanella floridae*
Flag Fish

51 *Aphyocharax*
rubripinnis
Bloodfin

52 *Hyphessobrycon flammeus*
Flame Tetra

53 *Metynnis roosevelti*

54 *Hemigrammus caudovittatus*
Tetra from
Buenos Aires

49

HEMIGRAMMUS caudovittatus Tetra from Buenos Aires   Plate 54

This is another beautiful characin, and is very easy to keep. It also likes to feed on plants. It is, however, a curious fact that this peculiarity is not manifest in all these fishes. The largest of this species will leave the plants alone. Can it be that the smaller ones lack something in their ordinary food so that they start eating things which they would not normally touch? Many people definitely give their fishes too little food, sometimes because they know no better, and sometimes through fear of overfeeding against which they are being constantly warned. If artificial food is given (I begin with this, because a beginner will start with it in spite of all advice to the contrary), then small portions only should be fed at a time. As a rule, the food does not contain that which a fish requires, so that some hobbyists start feeding vitamins, and no one yet knows whether a fish needs these. Bad, wrong, or insufficient food will keep the fish from growing. "Splendid" some folk may think, because the fish will then go well in a small tank; but they will not be strong and healthy. Incidentally, if the temperature is kept too high, above 75°F (24°C), this variety will remain small even though given good food.

HEMIGRAMMUS ocellifer Beacon or Head and Tail Light Fish   Plate 55

Now follows a series of really ideal aquarium fishes. The *ocellifer* comes from South America, and is also found in Surinam, in all kinds of water, and therefore it can stand a great deal, a matter of a great benefit to the beginner.

A small aquarium is quite large enough for this small species which will eat anything and everything, and look really beautiful. They also have an attractive popular name. They do not stir up dirt and do not eat plants and do not even snap at the fins of their fellows, while the breeding of them presents no difficulties. These grateful little fishes are certainly worth extra attention.

Keep them with a dark background consisting of beautiful slate rockery and a dark base with lacy *Myriophyllum* and *Cabomba* (plate 62). Have a shoal of them, consisting of some fifty fishes in an aquarium some 32 inches long and 16 inches wide and high. *Pistia stratiotes* a floating plant, with its long fine roots trailing in the water, is ideal for greenery. Have no other fishes with them and light them up from one corner and keep the room dark. Then sit and enjoy the sight and the silence, with maybe a very soft lilt of Spanish-American music. . . .

HEMIGRAMMUS nanus Silver Tips   Plate 56

This fish is usually known by its scientific name. People who are more versed in nomenclature than I am say it ought to be called *Hasemania melanura.* Given what is needs—and it is so well worth while—it will be a source of never-ending delight. It is content with very little, including a rather thinly populated aquarium which is not cleaned out too often, plenty of swimming space, some small fine greenery and a goodly planting around the sides. Three males and one or more females is an ideal population. When they have settled in, every male will take a bush of greenery as his particular private domain. If another male approaches, he will immediately come to investigate, with fins high for the attack, shuddering and shivering all over his body which appears in the most beautiful copper shimmer. The intruder will retire to his won territory with the other in pursuit, but this leads him on to the territory of number two, who will now attack in his turn. The result is that number one retreats to his own defined space and the roles are again reversed. They can provide endless entertainment. The females quickly find these exhibitionists, and the eggs are soon splashed around the plants.

PRISTELLA riddlei   Plate 57

It is extraordinary that such a popular little fish, so appreciated by many, still does not possess a popular name, even in America. Could it be because the scientific name sounds pretty and comes easily to the tongue?

Small wonder that it is so much liked by aquarium keepers everywhere. It has not got the amusing reflecting spots like the Head and Tail light fish, and it does not ply so amusingly as the Silver Tips, but the clear white spots on the fins immediately call attention to it, because in still water the fish will flex its fins again and yet again with swift jerks. Give this and the two preceding varieties a temperature of around 76°F (24°C).

Keep at least two pairs of them together and they will always be found in one another's company. These little characins are brilliant only in clear water. Never keep with them fishes which make a habit of stirring up mud. Neither rough or coarse plants suit them. A little morning sun is wonderful, especially if the surface of the water is covered with *Riccia,* which seems to have the gift of turning all the light that comes through into a lively green.

55 *Hemigrammus ocellifer*
Beacon or Head and Tail Light
Fish

56 *Hemigrammus
   nanus*
Silver Tips

57 *Pristella riddlei*

58 *Gymnocorymbus ternetzi*
Black Widow

59 *Moenkhausia sanctaefilomenae*
with
Echinodorus intermedius
Amazon Sword Plant

60 *Moenkhausia
pittieri*

53

GYMNOCORYMBUS ternetzi Black Widow Plate 58

The name Blackamour which this little fish received immediately upon its introduction into the aquarium world is also suitable, especially for the young ones. The tail end of the body, including the back and fins, is intensely jet black in all really good specimens. With older fishes, the black is apt to fade a little, especially if the temperatures are kept too high or fall too low; they really need a steady temperature of 68°F (20°C).

This is one of those types where quite a number should be kept in a bright green aquarium. No dark base, no dark rockeries, but everything well grown with bright and clear green plants. Several *Bacopa* species (Plate 18) will fit in well and look beautiful; there should be a good bottom growth of *Heteranthera zosteraefolia* (Plate 17) and one corner must be reserved for Eel grass (Plate 13).

Bloodfin Characin (Plate 51) make excellent company for them. They like just about the same temperature, and some *Heterandria formosa* should also be in the topmost layer of the water (Plate 1), in order to give the finishing touch to an aquarium needing very little work and giving a vast amount of satisfaction.

MOENKHAUSIA sanctæfilomenæ with Echinodorus intermedius Amazon Sword Plant Plate 59

This a much more sturdy characin than the previous ones, yet never grows much larger than $2^{1}/_{4}$ inches (and adult at that) in an aquarium. The red in the eyes is especially lively. The build of the body differs slightly from that of ordinary characin types. The coarse reflecting scales make this an attractive fish. Complaints have been made of plant-eating, but it must be remembered that this variety is a gourmand—a glutton. However, not only because of its plant eating, but also to make it appear more beautiful, only coarse plants should be found in its aquarium.

The Amazon Sword Plant in the picture is quite satisfactory and excellent on all points. It is a fine plant, but whether its scientific name is exactly correct, I should not like to say. It certainly is an *Echinodorus* but all these *Echinodorus* species have been crossed so often that they are no longer recognisable by the leaf shape only.

This plant should be given the company of sturdy and robust fishes such as Angel Fish (Plate 46), Mollie (Plate 9) and Swordtail (Plate 5).

54

MOENKHAUSIA pittieri   Plate 60

A diamond wedding is a union which has lasted for 60 years. Here in Plate 60 is the *Moenkhausia pittieri,* which on the Continent has been given the popular name of "Diamond" characin. I purposely chose it to close the series of easily-kept fishes. It is really a gem among aquarium specimens.

Every scale appears as though cut according to its own facet, so that the scales never reflect the light together, but with each movement different scales reflect light, exactly as do the facets of a well-cut diamond. This can be so fascinating that it is difficult to take one's eyes off the flashing lights. As we watch we reflect on the fact that our hobby also possesses many facets. Mind and body are kept occupied, a marvellous occupation for one's leisure time that few other hobbies afford. Only be sure that you keep the fishes and that the fishes do not start keeping you! That is to say, do not attempt to keep too many. The examples given speak for themselves: three to four different species in one tank, and sometimes only one kind. It is a mistake to try and keep too many in the aquarium, or the time might come when you would not have time to enjoy the hobby. One is able to give proper time and attention to a few fishes and to learn more from them.

Pterophyllum scalare
Angel Fish (see no. 46)

Natural food

Gnat larva (*Culex*)   *Chironomid larva*

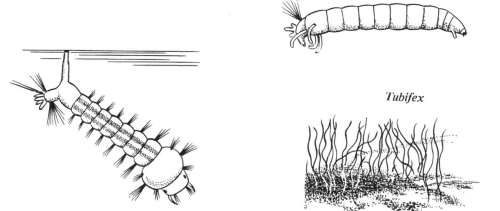

Tubifex

One of the best live foods for aquarium fishes is the water-flea *Daphnia,* a small crustacean. At the right season they are abundant in pools, and pet-shops generally keep a stock of them.

Gnat larvae (*Culex*) may be found hanging from the surface-film of a pond, or even a water-butt, by a little breathing tube, for they need air. They are related to mosquitoes, but do not carry malaria parasites.

Chironomid midges belong to another family. The larvae of some species have red blood, which shows through the thin integument and gives them the name of "blood-worms". Near the hind end are some blood-gills that permit the oxygen to diffuse into the blood so that they can live at the bottom of the pond, lake or stream.

Tubifex is a small red worm that burrows in the slimy mud of rather foul water, leaving its hind end waving in the water, to aerate its blood. They may now be obtained freeze-dried.

PART TWO

SPECIES WHICH NEED SPECIAL CARE

PART TWO

Species which need special care

There are so many species of fishes to be found in aquaria that it would, of course, be impossible to show them all here.

In this part I shall discuss a number of species which need special care, and to keep which it is necessary to take great trouble. Some are difficult to acquire, some are difficult to rear and some need more attention to keep them alive. Breeding is not always easy, and in some cases may be very difficult. Certain species have never yet been bred in captivity; others, again, are notoriously difficult. If success attends your efforts, that is a spur to further attempts. The more difficulties we have to overcome, the greater our sense of attainment.

In Part One, I was not enthusiastic about the community tank. The fishes which I shall describe now belong still less to the company of others and generally each comes from an entirely different surrounding. There are fantastic specialities here, so much so that those people who hitherto have learned little about fishes are in for many surprises. Surprise will, I hope, turn eventually, to admiration. There is not only beauty of colour, shape and movement to admire, but also beauty of organization. In addition there is the spirit of man, which has been able to discover how everything fits in and works to such perfection.

Some larger fishes are almost barred from aquaria, because they will eat the smaller ones. A big specimen like the *Cichlasoma meeki* which is shown on the large picture (Plate 121), cannot be kept with little ones, so we see it only in aquaria of the Zoological Gardens or, in a rare case, a private aquarium.

These large fishes are usually fairly easy to keep, as they make few demands on the composition of the water. On the other hand, some of the small fishes are fastidious. Here and there comments will be made about "soft water"; "acid water"; "brackish or low salt content". I shall discuss these matters, so that we may know how best to deal with them.

That there is a difference between hard and soft water is, I suppose, obvious to everyone. We have all experienced this difference when we have washed our hands with ordinary soap; sometimes when the water is hard, we can soften it by adding soda or borax.

The presence of lime or magnesium salts makes the water hard. In some areas the water is mostly soft; in the chalk areas it is hard.

Sea-water also contains many other salts, including lime and magnesium. That is because rainwater on its way from the mountains to the sea has absorbed salts from the soil and carried them seawards. The seawater evaporates, but the salts remain. The evaporated water makes clouds which again fall on the earth as snow or rain or hail. This water once more finds its way into brooks and rivers, and more salts are absorbed and are carried gradually down to the sea.

When the rainwater passes over areas which in former ages were inland seas, it takes up much of the salts deposited there.

With the sea all around Britain, it is obvious that many places will have hard water. Indeed, it is difficult to understand how soft water is on tap at all in some districts. Wherever we see heather or rhododendrons growing wild, we may be fairly certain that there is no lime in the soil and hence none in the water. No one quite knows why one plant cannot tolerate lime and why another thrives on it, but it is the same with fishes.

If a certain plant thrives only where the soil contains lime, it stands to reason that that plant needs lime in the soil. In the same way all plants take up salts and convert them to their own use. When the vegetation dies off, a great percentage of those salts returns to the soil, but not all in such a way that they are easily soluble in rainwater. When a sandy soil has had a thick layer of humus deposited on top of it through the centuries by dead plants falling and decomposing, it is likely that streams passing through it will contain little or no lime; they will consist of soft water but many other things will be absorbed, and hence the water may be brownish in colour. This is different from rainwater, or from water newly released from the snows and cheerfully making its appearance as a leaping and bounding rivulet, both of which are soft.

Water containing soda is also soft, but this type of softness is quite different from the others.

I have just referred to the humus of centuries and that causes us to think at once of forest land. The moors are really identical, though the soil is composed of the humus of different plants. Hence, though similar in character, it is vastly different chemically.

Peat has the property of making the water acid. If we trickle our tap water through well-washed peat, it will become acid.

Some chemicals can be used to remove the salts from water. Here is a real miracle, that, from water containing salts, there remains only water which has been softened and de-salted. The necessary chemicals are obtainable from reliable dealers in aquarium requisites. Such water, poor in salt content, is necessary for some fishes, at least while they are very young, though we do not known why. In this way we can make entirely salt-less water. It might be thought easier to collect rainwater but this may contain a multitude of undesirable elements.

We can buy distilled water; that is certainly good. But we may just as well

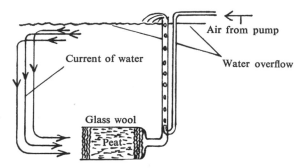

start by buying the necessary apparatus for treating the ordinary tap water.

If the fishes require water to be merely acid and not necessarily poor in salts, we can make good use of the sphagnum moss or even of peat. The pieces of peat must be pulled apart and everything boiled up in order to remove hard lumps and bits of stalk and impurities.

We can make a nice thick layer of peat treated in this way, over a well-washed sandy bottom, which is lime-free. We can check this by adding a few drops of hydrochloric acid to the sand. If it fizzes, it is not yet right for our purpose. This peat makes the bottom look very dark, forms a wonderful foil for many fishes, and creates a marvellous effect.

We can also use a peat filter; to work this we must buy a little pump. It is possible to make the peat filter ourselves, but it is on sale. The drawing clearly shows how it works. The air pumped through the thin tube draws water into the wide tube where it falls over the top back into the water of the aquarium. This water on the way passes through some glass wool, then through the fine peat before it enters the wide tube. The whole apparatus can be camouflaged by pieces of slate and plants. Care must be taken with the rockery; marble, or limestone cannot be used, but quartz is excellent. Acid water must not come into contact with any metal parts.

I have only at this stage mentioned a pump. It is good for the dealer that everyone seems to want one of these bubbly things in his or her aquarium. Many people seem to think that an aquarium without a pump is not a finished article. Did you ever see a pump in a brook or a ditch? Marsh gas may escape from the bottom of a pool here and there, but never with such an eternal stream of bubbles. If it is necessary to remove excess carbon dioxide from the tank, then the aquarium is either over-populated or not well-planted. In other words, we try, just as we do with human illness, to treat the symptoms rather than to remove the cause. We reach for cough mixture or nasal drops in case of a cough or a cold; but they do not cure the illness, though they may allay the symptoms.

63

It really is a very remarkable attitude to take to life, not to look for the root cause, but to try and alter the results.

Let us not act so foolishly with our aquarium. I am not now referring to the treatment of our fishes, but rather am I advising on how we can prevent illness.

Newly-acquired fishes should not be placed immediately in an already populated tank. Keep them apart for a few days in a separate aquarium. Do not even put them straightaway into what I would call a quarantine tank. The water in which the newly-acquired fishes have been living previously probably was of a different chemical composition from the water in their new living quarters. The sudden change-over could prove fatal. Add the new water little by little to the water in which they are at present so that, in a few hours' time, with a slow transition, they may be prepared for your aquarium. In this way the change of temperature will not be too great, though that is not anything like so important as the changed character of the water.

Look out for the tap water supplied by your Water Board. Some Boards have added chemicals to the water to such an extent that fishes (as well as your house plants) may die. If in doubt, state your problem to the Water Board.

If the fishes thrive in the quarantine tank, accustom them again very slowly to the water of the aquarium in which you intend to keep them.

Watch your plants. If they no longer grow, then things may go wrong with your fishes as well. The reason may be found in the first introduction; not enough light, not enough manure. Sometimes the surface plants will grow so fast that they take away the light from the plants at the bottom. The close growth will also interfere with the circulation of the water so that, while the top layer may be excellent, the bottom layers may be no longer suitable. Sometimes we shall notice that some fishes will start swimming in the upper layers, which formerly they did not do.

If, therefore, we know the habits of our fishes, because we have so often watched them, then we see very quickly if something is wrong.

Take care that there is quiet in the aquarium. In the first place: no overcrowding; and in the second place: time for sleep! I cannot supply figures for overcrowding. The dwarfs in Plate 1 have sufficient room given one quart of water each (four to the gallon) but an Electric Eel of three feet in length needs a great deal more. As soon as the aquarium looks like a wriggling mass, something is seriously wrong!

Then there is sleep. Fishes do not have eyelids and cannot close their eyes. But they most certainly sleep. Just switch on the light suddenly above the aquarium. Those fishes will look so different; the *Neon tetra* in Plate 71 are suddenly no longer blue, the Angel Fish no longer black; the *Nannostomus* in Pate 78 have the most curious black cross bands, and so on.

LIMNOPHILA species   Plate 61

Very many species of the *Limnophila* are known.

For many years they were called *Ambulia*. They are difficult to determine on the leaf shape alone. Which type is pictured here is hard to say with any certainty and therefore I have used as a heading "species". This is often found abbreviated to "spec.".

The former *Ambulia* was once found in almost every aquarium. A beautiful clear green; it was an easy plant to grow and we could take cuttings ad lib. Suddenly, however, complaints began to arise. In the same aquarium where it had always flourished, and for years at a time, it suddenly went wrong. In more recent years *Ambulia* has been thriving better, but the question arises: Is this a difficult plant?

61 *Limnophila* species

SYNODONTIS nigriventris with Cabomba caroliniana Upside Down Catfish
Plate 62

At an Antwerp exhibition I saw the fish in this picture for the first time. Although the typical can swim in the ordinary way, this one normally, and it seems for preference, swims upside-down. It is equipped for that, for its belly

62 *Synodontis nigriventris* with *Cabomba caroliniana*
Upside Down Catfish

is darker (hence the name "Black Belly") than its back; in this respect it is the opposite to other fishes. It dives into every nook and cranny hunting for bits and pieces, preferably carrion, so that a dead fish, which has disappeared at the back somewhere, is soon disposed of. In a way, that is very useful. If there are, as I sincerely hope, no dead fishes in your tank, feed the "Black Belly" a little lean beef or liver (raw of course). He does not seem to appreciate live food.

The fan leaf shown here is met with in many stagnant or slow running streams in North and South Carolina, flowering in mid-summer with white blossoms touched with yellow. This is a plant which can be difficult. It needs considerable light to get it to bloom and good feeding is appreciated. Good loam at the roots is advisable. Cuttings are easily taken if we pinch the stalk underneath the spot where the axil bud has developed.

CRYPTOCORYNE griffithi   Plate 63

The *Cryptocoryne* are plants which, in their country of origin (that is India, Malaya and the Indonesian Archipelago), live submerged for part of the year only in order to grow, during the dry season, above the water and flower. This proves that they are real bog lovers. If we plant them on the bottom of our tanks, that is rather unnuatural, and if they only get well washed sand to grow in they have difficulty in keeping alive. They may stay just alive even whith a minimum of light but they do not grow. This is not a group which can be used and depended on to take much carbon dioxide from the water and to furnish oxygen.

We can help them a little by mixing some good leaf mould with the sand and leaving them alone (they should not be transplanted unnecessarily). Then they will develop into beautiful plants. There are many species which are to be found in aquaria.

The two illustrated are somewhat similar plants to those in other plates as, for instance, the *Cryptocoryne affinis*. These plants can be expensive to buy, yet I would advise the purchase of two plants of every variety when it is possible.

CRYPTOCORYNE nevelli with Hyphessobrycon pulchripinnis Lemon Tetra
Plate 64

These plants will bring green, brown and reddish colours into the aquarium. They are very easy to keep and they need not be pruned, like the *Heteranthera, Bacopa, Limnophila,* and *Cabomba.* They slowly develop into a close bush, so that the sandy soil is no longer visible. The little fishes show up beautifully in such surroundings.

66

When the fish shown here (popularly known as Lemon Tetra) is above washed sharp sand, the fine yellow lemon colour cannot be seen. With all those mixed colours of greens, browns and reds, half a dozen of these fishes make a wonderful sight. There are many aquarium keepers whose sole aim is to keep *Cryptocorynes* and small *Characin*, of which Lemon Tetra is one.

HYPHESSOBRYCON rosaceus   Plate 65

HYPHESSOBRYCON callistus "Minor"   Plate 66

Either of these two fishes in Plates 65 and 66 fits wonderfully well into a tank of *Cryptocorynes*. But in one of the standard works on aquarium fishes it is suggested that it is practically impossible that they should be two species, suggesting they are really two varieties of one species. This would be proof that in varied circumstances animals of one species may develop in different fashions and that those differences can be, or will be, hereditary. The long black fin of the male *rosaceus* does not develop in the case of the "Minor". The spawn of the "Minor" hatch very quickly, sometimes after only 14 hours, while the eggs of the *rosaceus* generally take thirty hours before the little fishes put in an appearance.

Rosaceus is found only in the farthest north of South America, viz. in the basin of the Surinam river, while the "Minor" is found in much more southerly latitudes. *Rosaceus* can have even during the breeding, a little lime in the water, which need not be very soft. "Minor", on the contrary, must have soft water, but it may not be acid. This "Minor" is, therefore, much more difficult in the breeding.

Furthermore, the fry are so very small. Consequently their food must also be minute. For early days infusoria from a nearby ditch is certainly required. We must take it with a very fine nylon net mesh from "healthy" water and from near reeds if possible. You can get advice about the size of the net from the dealer, or from your aquarium club. Later on, when the little fishes have grown, or are even mature, live food is still a necessity. Some types will accustom themselves to very finely grated raw meat, and will grow fantastically fast on this diet. Care must be taken not to introduce small snails, especially pond snails which should not be used owing to the danger of introducing a parasite worm (which will cause thick eyes and finally blindness). One of the Corydoras could be used for scavenging purposes. The tanks sometimes suffer from the disadvantage that the rotting processes close to the bottom no longer work according to plan, and instead of nitrate emerging as an end product, a nitrite is formed which means a speedy death to many fishes.

63 *Cryptocoryne griffithi*

64 *Cryptocoryne nevelli* with
Hyphessobrycon pulchripinnis
Lemon Tetra

HYPHESSOBRYCON heterorhabdus
(Known on the Continent as Belgian Flag)
Plate   67
Red-yellow and black—these colours are
so evident on this truly striking little

65 *Hyphessobrycon rosaceus*

66 *Hyphessobrycon callistus*
Minor

(Plate 67 cont'd)

fish. It might be expected to be present in all the Benelux countries (Netherlands, Belgium and Luxemburg). But this is not the case; it is extremely rare, and it is an extremely sensitive fish. Breeding is not difficult if the temperature is kept high enough—83°F (28°C.). Yet there are many victims during the rearing period. The breeding tank needs to be fairly large, otherwise the fry may die at the first ditch water administered. Either the changes of chemical constitution of the water, or the variation in temperature, may prove to be fatal. A sudden decomposition of dead food stuff often causes the first deaths.

Yet strangely enough, I have seen these fishes looking very beautiful in hard water, in soft water, in acid water and in water deficient in salts. The essential thing is to accustom them very gradually to the water in the aquarium. This point must be watched when acquiring new fishes of this and other species which are equally sensitive. The vessel in which they are moved must have in it the actual water from the tank in which they have been swimming.

67 *Hyphessobrycon heterorhabdus*
(known on the Continent as Belgian Flag)

69

ANOPTICHTHYS jordani Blind Cave Fish Plate 68

In some caves in Yugoslavia live the Proteus. They are gilled salamanders, which have not developed their eyes: In the wonderful Mammoth caverns in Kentucky, America (which have been declared as National Park), there lives a fish without eyes: it closely resembles a species of dog-fish found in waters outside the caves. Mexico has similar stalactite caves and it is there that the Blind Cave Fish is found, which so much resembles the *Astyanax mexicanus* living in the rivers outside the caves, that it is easy to assume that the blind type has evolved from the normal.

The guides in the Kentucky caves have made it a custom to extinguish the light after the trip, which lasts some four hours. Then visitors realise what darkness is, they peer and peer and can distinguish nothing at all. That positively hurts the eyes, and they naturally close to ease the strain. Then the pain disappears. These fishes are spared that pain, the useless staring is finished, but the collateral organs with which the water pressure is gauged are much more strongly developed. Never allow this variety to be worried by other fishes in the aquarium. We cannot provide it with anything like natural surroundings, neither with running water nor darkness.

CARNEGIELLA strigata Hatchet Fish Plate 69

The more we observe animals, the clearer it becomes that every species is equipped with exactly what is needed for its special surroundings and circumstances. The Hatchet Fish, one of three which can be easily obtained, has a keel like a fast cruiser. It seems as though it has to clear the surface and it does so. This species is very definitely a flying fish. This *strigata* can be accustomed to all manner of food, but if there are little flies above the surface of the water, the fishes will soon begin their gliding jumps and care must be taken that they do not crash into the light hood or the sides of the aquarium. Such a crash might prove fatal.

I wish that some fanciers would specialise in the hatchet fishes. They have not even been bred yet with any measure of success. They should be housed in a very large aquarium where the sides above the water could be lined with foam plastic. They should be given a piece of sandy beach as well as a rocky, pebbly beach with bog plants, in order to provide for spawning.

HEMIGRAMMUS erythrozonus Glow Light Tetra Plate 70

HYPHESSOBRYCON innesi Neon Tetra Plate 71

It was during the summer of 1936 that the Frenchman A. Rabout penetrated the jungles of South America on the borders of Brazil and Columbia, and there found in the shallow creeks and bogs the little fishes shown on Plate 71.

Is it surprising that this man, who only a few months before had seen the lights of the advertisements in Paris, was reminded of them by seeing this fluorescent blue and bright red?

They are extremely popular; everyone seems to have them, which proves that they must be tolerably strong little fishes. It is only the breeding that presents difficulties. The eggs will not hatch if the water does not resemble those dark, wooded, pools, practically without living plants but with decomposed vegetation, which formed their natural habitat.

The water in these pools was slightly acid and free from lime. It is, therefore, logical that even beginners in this hobby can breed this little fish, if they live in a well-wooded area and collect their water from ponds or streams by the woods. The water should be kept at 75°F (24°C) and salt dissolved in it facilitates breeding.

Whilst the Glow Light Tetra in Plate 70, often described by the scientific name of *Hyphessobrycon gracilis,* needs warmer water, the Neon Tetra requires 68°F (20°C).

These fishes should not, at all events, be kept above a clean base. A clear floor is not suitable. A decorative piece of old wood, well-boiled, makes the background they need. Very fine *Myriophyllum* only should be added as plants. Soft water, which will soon take on a yellow tinge through the piece of wood, is also necessary, and light should not be allowed in from the side or back windows.

CTENOBRYCON spilurus Silver Tetra   Plate 72

Why is it that we meet this Silver Tetra only very sporadically? Admittedly it is a voracious devourer of spawn, but others also err in that respect. Is it only because it is larger than the other Characin? Or it is because it will also devour plants like the large *Metynnis roosevelti* (Plate 53)? It does, indeed, somewhat resemble this fish at first sight, but I was never troubled by its eating of healthy plants.

How beautiful these large disc-like fish slide through the water. In a big tank, more than 3 feet long, it is a brilliant sight to see these fishes which, when alone, are so slothful, dart around in playful flight. A bright green tank is recommended with a few varieties of *Cabomba, Valisneria gigantea* and some floating greenery. A clean bright base is needed and preferably some hours of sunshine during the morning and a fairly high temperature around 77°F (25°C). These fishes do best in a long established tank with a superfluity of plants. They seem to like dead food, even dead vegetation, decomposed for preference. Leaves from plants which die off and fall are especially fancied.

68 *Anoptichthys
jordani*
Blind Cave Fish

69 *Carnegiella
strigata*
Hatchet Fish

70 *Hemigrammus
erythrozonus*
Glow Light Tetra

72

71 *Hyphessobrycon innesi*
Neon Tetra

72 *Ctenobrycon spilurus*
Silver Tetra

THAYERIA sanctaemariae (obliqua) Penguin Fish   Plate 73

The name *obliqua* is derived from the obliquely downward turn of the back line as it passes through the tail fin. On the Continent this fish is sometimes popularly called the "Hockeystick".

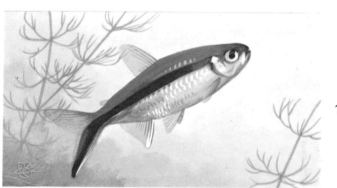

73 *Thayeria obliqua*
Penguin Fish

Why is it that this little fish, when at rest in the water, always hangs in this oblique fashion? Again, I must admit that I do not know, and have never been able to find out from others who have kept it. We do know, however, that the swimming bladder does not reach to the end of the fish, as with the related *characin*. The fish, therefore, behaves as if it had bladder inflammation.

It has often been noticed that a fish which always drops its tail suddenly tries to jerk its body into a normal horizontal line. The inflammation may be caused by a too low temperature of the water, which lessens the resistance of the fish to disease. If these infections occur, the temperature of the water should be raised, close watch being kept meanwhile to see that no distress is caused to the fishes, and that they do not swim to the surface for air. In these circumstances the temperature may be as high as 92°F (33°C).

The "hockeysticks" always swim crookedly; when at rest they are absolutely lopsided, but do not jerk themselves into the horizontal with one movement.

HEMMIGRAMMUS unilineatus Feather Fin   Plate 74

During the 1920's every aquarium keeper had a set of these Feather Fins. They were popular because they resembled the smaller and much more beautiful *Pristella riddlei* (Plate 57); they were also easier to keep because they were stronger and able to withstand all manner of minor ailments. Breeding was very easy, and they were recognised as being grateful little fishes.

But the fanciers were not so grateful. They soon tired of this variety and desired smaller fishes more brightly coloured and more expensive.

To-day I should be surprised if one hundred fanciers can be found who still keep them. Even then they may possibly not be of first rate quality, for generations of them have had insufficient care and attention.

I once received a malformed pair bred from them, and all the off-spring were absolutely normal. Just like the "hockeystick" they prefer shallow water of 77°F (25°C) and some floating green. During the mating season the males are apt to be agressive; this points to the fact that they do not breed in a shoal.

CORYNOPOMA riisei Swordtail Characin   Plate 75

This silver-grey characin, which does not possess an adipose fin like the rest of the family, has been known for a long while under the name of *Stevardia albipinnis*. Now not only has the name been changed, but the fish as well, for instead of the grey fishes we now meet only an albino form which lacks most of its pigmentation, without having obtained another colouring in compensation. In this way it has become quite a striking little fish, especially if it is kept in dark surroundings which are its natural habitat.

It is not difficult to keep; it can live in hard and soft water, poor in salt, to

74

brackish; everything seems to agree with it but it prefers temperatures varying between 58°F and 86° F (14-30° C).

Its breeding is very peculiar. The female lays fertilised eggs, but how does this happen? Does the male use the spoonlike projection of the gills plate? He does indeed swing about with these, very importantly, during the mating movements. The transport of the seed is simplified; there is no milting but a capsule of spermatozoa, a so-called spermatophore. The latest literature on the subject state that the spermatophore is brought across not by the spoons but by the belly fin. I have never seen it happen myself.

PHENACOGRAMMUS interruptus Congo Characin   Plate 76

There are multitudes of fishes in the immeasurable river basins of the Congo; but this is the first species to receive the attention of aquarium fanciers, and therefore is honoured by the name of Congo Characin.

It is not surprising that amateurs are interested in it. It needs to be seen in very dark surroundings—a peaty bottom and dark stones. With a good bushy growth of bright green plants, a wonderful green reflection on those gloriously glistening scales is conjured up. The peat makes the water soft and slightly acid.

In those circumstances it is a strong fish, which grows to mature beauty. The male has a chalk-white edge to his slovenly-grown tail fin. He becomes large, but this is no disadvantage in his case. Everyone likes to possess this species, but breeding is anything but simple. The water has to be fairly strongly acid and poor in salts for that particular purpose; a thick layer of peat-moss litter is then a necessity. For the growing fry, and slightly larger fishes, I would strongly advise the use of a peat filter.

POECILOBRYCON auratus Pencil Fish   Plate 77

In Plate 73 there is a fish hanging lop-sided; this one is standing almost upright on its tail, star-gazing. A single specimen seems amusing, but a careful study in a tank, filled with ribbon-like plants, shows that these movements are something more than amusing; they have a design. One can scarcely see these fishes, even from the side, but above, where the herons and other birds are out for prey, it is well-nigh impossible to spot them. They move so gently from place to place that they cannot be readily recognised. These little fishes are fairly strong; a single pair will not be particularly interesting, because they so seldom show themselves. It is necessary to have a separate aquarium for them, with bog plants such as *Acorus pusillus* or some rushes and to provide the acid surroundings which this fish appreciates so much. Larvae of the ordinary mosquito make ideal food, as their little mouths can just manage to deal with fully-grown mosquito larvae.

NANNOSTOMUS anomalus

Golden Pencil Fish   Plate 78

The word "anomalus", of course, refers to the lack of the adipose fin.

The name "beckfordi" has sometimes been used.

The general shape and markings suggest that this fish must be related to the Pencil Fish; this is correct, though the latter possesses the adipose fin.

There is yet another similarity. Both species show a totally different colouring and marking by night than by day. Very large black marks on the gill plates and flanks make it look like a different fish. Is it nature's camouflage on a moonlight night?

74 *Hemigrammus unilineatus*
Feather Fin

I have never yet swum in shallow water on a tropical night, wearing a diver's helmet, and feeling my way between the luxurious growth of plants in the waters of the northern parts of South America, but I can believe that marauders have to be guarded against and small fishes have to take care not to come too close to snapping mouths!

It should be kept warm at 83°F (28°C).

75 *Corynopoma riisei*
Swordtail Characin

76

76 *Phenacogrammus interruptus*
Congo Characin

77 *Poecilobrycon auratus*
Pencil Fish

78 *Nannostomus anomalus*
Golden Pencil Fish

CORYDORAS arcuatus with Ludwigia alternefolia   Plate 79

This little catfish like the *paleatus* is a small vacuum cleaner. But this one does not make such a mess in the tank. Nor do *Corydoras hastatus, myersi* and *melanistius*. They are all bold aquarium occupants which do not hide by day to the same extent as the *paleatus* and the *punctatus*. They all know how to find the small decomposing pieces of foodstuff and to clear them up as good little scavengers should. As they are also beautiful, they are of advantage to keep in an aquarium.

Why then is it that we see them so infrequently? Possibly it is because they are not too easy to breed. They need a thick layer of peat moss litter in the slightly acid, soft water. The best plan is to have a number of males and one female ready to spawn. All those males will make life troublesome for the lonely female, but this is necessary. At long last one male succeeds in attaching himself to her abdomen, in such a way that the ventral fins of the male and female touch. When she lays the eggs, she holds them with her ventral fin for a little while, then the male milts them and lets her go. She swims to a piece of wood or something similar, in order to glue her eggs (never more than ten in number) there. This conduct is repeated several times; it resembles the mating of frogs.

NEOLEBIAS ansorgii   Plate 80

Although this little fish is like a tench, it is a *citharinid* and hails from the Congo. I discuss it in company with the *Corydoras* because this fish also grubs along the bottom for rotting material of vegetable and animal origin. Because it is always scrabbing and scavinging among the plants we donot often see it. If, however, we sit quitly in front of a well-planted aquarium and this little fish suddenly puts in an appearance, moving slowly forward, then we are immediately attracted by it. If the fish is kept in an "acid" aquarium, healthy and warm, the green gloss on its body will look beautiful. The fish will seem so distinctive that it will immediately attract attention.

Though perhaps I should not say so, it also looks friendly and kind. A dark coloured bottom will make the most effective foil to its colouring. Peat moss litter finely divided is good for it, while a peat filter, though not an absolute necessity, is advisable if we ever should consider breeding.

Although nothing appertaining to shoal formation is ever noticed, the breeding seems to be facilitated if a certain number of males and females are kept together. As with the *Corydoras* a thick layer of peat on the bottom of the tank is essential.

COPEINA arnoldi   Plate 81

Both these *Copeina* species though fairly large, are ideal aquarium inhabitants. They are elegant, colourful and lively. They can nearly always be found in the top layer of the water. Although they are characins, they lack the adipose fin, though the young fishes still show it. They are especially interesting on account of their almost unbelievable reproduction. This can only be observed with the *arnoldi* if a strong, smooth, leaf or glass slide is fixed at a height of 1 to 1½ inches above the water.

The male, with his beautiful dorsal fin and bright colours, vaults as though inspecting the places against the lower side of the preferably horizontal smooth surface, which he touches with his belly. If there is a ripe female, we soon see her approach the male and, after an agitated swimming hither and thither, they both leap towards the smooth surface where the female attached her eggs by some adhesive mass. Instantly the eggs are fertilised by the male. The fishes cannot, of course, retain this position for more than a fraction of a second; they will fall back into the water, repeat the leap and action, and another batch of the eggs are laid. These are deposited, not on top of the others, but by the side of them. In this way a hundred or more eggs may be laid. The female then leaves but the male remains in the neighbourhood of the spawn which he guards and saves from drying out by splashing the eggs every quarter of an hour or so with several rapid lashings of his tail fin. A really marvellous piece of natural history.

Who would ever think of fishes laying their eggs outside the water? But they are wonderfully safeguarded against egg-devourers that live in the water.

COPEINA guttata   Plate 82

The *guttata* also safeguards its eggs.

The *guttata* pair will make a hole in the sand, where the future parents turn and twist, one behind the other, in a fairly small circle. The small eggs are laid in groups of twenty or thirty, until maybe a thousand eggs have been deposited. The male guards the eggs for a few days and seems even to cleanse them with his mouth. They generally hatch on the third day and then the best way is to give them plenty of room.

BARBUS titteya Cherry Barb   Plate 83

Most of the Barbs are exceptionally easy aquarium fishes as we have already noticed in Part One. Here follow two more, which are considerably more

79

79 *Corydoras arcuatus* with
  Ludwigia alternefolia

80 *Neolebias ansorgii*

(Plate 83 cont'd)

difficult, but they are worth perseverance for they are so beautiful; no picture is really adequate to illustrate them. The Cherry Barb is very different in shape from the species already discussed. In fact, so far as appearance goes, it resembles the large Barb which is so prolific in France and is caught there by rod-and-line with a grape as bait.

In Ceylon, the Cherry Barb lives in shallow warmish water with plenty of vegetation. The tank needs a temperature around 86°F (30°C.), and plenty of plants, so that the bushiness of the greenery does not allow any fierce sunrays to reach the bottom. In its natural surroundings this fish will live on a rich supply of decomposing plant material, together with a muddy bottom covered by a brown mass of rotting leaves, and with lots of bacteria infusoria and other unicellular life. The fish will live on the bacteria and mosquito larvae, and will feed in turn on the unicellular organisms. Just imagine what this fish would lack in a newly-planted aquarium, with only sharp sand on the bottom. It is advisable to buy these fishes only when your tank is well-established, preferably old and heavily overgrown with plants.

81 *Copeina arnoldi*

82 *Copeina guttata*

83 *Barbus titteya*
Cherry Barb

BARBUS tetrazona Tiger Barb   Plate 84

This flamboyant fish possesses unusually high spirits, but it finds a ready sale at the dealers. Individual specimens are sometimes very badly developed. A good *tetrazona* should be 2¼ inches long and have a velvety gloss on its black stripe and a well-rounded body.

All too often the fishes will not grow after they have been bought. The belly is no longer rounded and the black colouring has become matt and dull. Then the complaints start. For a time these fish will act strangely almost standing on their heads. Then this phase will pass off, only to begin again a week later. This strange behaviour may last for only five minutes and will disappear without fatal consequences. Nevertheless fishes may be found lying dead in the tank with no clue to infection or damage. The *tetrazona* cannot stand a clean tank. It needs exactly similar surroundings to those described for the *titteya* with a lower temperature and acid water (peat-filter).

Do not put angel fishes with *tetrazonas,* for the latter are persistent fin nibblers. The fine long fins of the angel fish would disappear.

MARSILEA quadrifolia Four-leaved Clover   Plate 85

With the two previous pictures I recommend a closely-planted tank. This plant is particularly suitable for such a tank, where it is completely at home. It is really a fern, and does not always live submerged. Those nurseries which grow it for the market, in order to obtain as many plants as possible in the shortest time, use bog-like surrounding; muddy soil with a bare inch of water.

Now we force it to live on the bottom of an aquarium. If the water is deep enough, say, 16 inches, it behaves normally, but if the water is only 8 inches deep it will develop a number of leaves on very tall stems which will not manage to reach the surface, but the plant will lose all its attractiveness.

If there is a lot of light, these plants will soon become covered by algae and will pine away and die. An acid condition suits them best; therefore, a peat aquarium is the correct place for them. The brownish colour of the water caused by the peat prevents too much light from penetrating down to and making them too robust and vigorous.

RASBORA trilineata Scissors Tail   Plate 86

This is a strong little fish which fortunately is still met quite frequently. Perhaps I should have discussed this species in the first part of this book, but I preferred not to do so; firstly because other and more difficult *Rasbora* will follow here, and secondly, because the "Scissors Tail" also presents a few difficulties.

It is a little fish which always moves in large shoals, and also reproduces whole shoals at a time. I have heard that in the island of Sumatra it can usually be found in muddy, mainly acid, waters, but at certain times of the year not a single fish can be spotted in those waters. This seems to point to migration and possibly the search for a home with different chemical characteristics.

We cannot supply these fishes with that, and this may possibly account for the failure to breed. But I have also noticed a pair start to breed when a couple of mirrors were set up, and the reflections suggested the presence of a number of fish. That may be worthwhile remembering if we want to attempt breeding. These fishes should be given a large tank with muddy bottom and slightly acid water. They will live together with Tiger Barb, provided there is plenty of room to move.

The plant illustrated here is the Indian Water Pest, *Hydrilla verticillata*.

RASBORA maculata   Plate 87

Jewels are seldom large and at their best only in a good setting; similarly with these small fishes. They should be kept in a tank darkened with pieces of peat moss litter which have first of all been pulled apart and well boiled. If we can find an elegantly-shaped branch from a pond, we can also boil this up well and place it in the aquarium. Eel grass or tape grass in one corner and a veritable wood of *Cryptocorynes* (see Plates 63 and 64) make a suitable setting.

A little sunshine is needed in the tank during the morning. This species should not be given large fishes for company.

In the picture they are shown with *Cabomba*. This plant does not grow in their actual natural habitat, but it will and does grow in similar conditions. In this way we can keep natives of America with those from Africa and Asia, if only we ensure that all of them come from similar surroundings.

The *Rasbora maculata* does well in company with the Lemon Tetra (plate 64) with *Hemigrammus erythrozonus* (Plate 71) and *Poecilobrycon auratus* (Plate 77).

Breeding is not simple because the fry definitely require soft, slightly acid water. I cannot advise attempts to breed with a single pair only.

RASBORA heteromorpha   Plate 88

This little fish is very beautiful and also very strong. Its name means "varying in shape". It can be kept in all kinds of water, though it is doubtful whether it is wise to do so. This is probably why no one seems to succeed in breeding this species. Naturally the fault is looked for elsewhere. This has given rise to the tale that in the neighbourhood of Singapore only male fishes were sold, because the distinction in sex is most difficult to determine. I have been told, that the males have a distinctly lighter stripe above the cone-shaped spot, while the females only have a vague indication there. But I was never able to confirm that statement.

83

84 *Barbus tetrazona*

85 *Marsilea quadrifolia*
Four-leaved Clover

As can be seen from the illustration this plant spreads in strawberrylike fashion by means of runners. It can be propagated by dividing the root and replanting the pieces.

(Plate 88 cont'd.)

It is comparatively easy to breed in slightly acid, limeless, surroundings. A number of pairs should be allowed to mate together. The females will attach their eggs to the underside of large-leaved *Cryptocoryne*.

These little fishes will combine well with *Barbus tetrazona* (Plate 84) and small type of *Characin*. Mosquito larvae make the best food for them.

86 *Rasbora trilineata*
Scissors Tail

87 *Rasbora maculata*

88 *Rasbora heteromorpha*

ACANTHOPHTHALMUS semicinctus Coolie   Plate 89

We are familiar with the Loaches from our own waters, *Cobitis,* the small Loach from the low lying grounds, and *Nemacheilus,* the Loach found in our brooks. Some never grub in the mud and none have jaw teeth. But the smallest species like mud. A low barometric pressure will make them gasp for breath and they will swallow that air and therefore they can still exist when other fish die.

This species behaves exactly like our little mud loaches. It will always be in the ground, except when barometric pressure changes. Hence do not keep it on a floor with sharp sand, which would prevent its digging in, but provide a mud bottom with an addition of peat moss litter, a few flat stones to hide under, and a thick planting to scrabble between and around, hunting for worms and dead material. Breeding has been successful only twice to my knowledge; this little fish is fairly rare. Soft acid water is essential to induce breeding.

HYPOSTOMUS plecostomus   Plate 90

This fish is an even greater lover of darkness than the previous one; it is visible only in a good tank, lit up suddenly during the evening. A fish which always lies hidden under a sizable slab of stone during the day seems pointless in an aquarium but it is one of the really good consumers of algae. It will eat the much dreaded blue algae even better than the Kissing Gourami or the *Mollienisia* types (Part One) which are also recommended for this purpose.

The *plecostomus* has its mouth absolutely designed so as to scrape off the algae from flat stones or strong leaves or from the glass of aquaria.

With that mouth, these fishes attach themselves to the stones and rocks in the rapids of their native rivers. They normally prefer the rapids, as do the *Otocinclus* and the *Loricaria.* We can also use the latter in the aquarium for the same scavanging purposes.

All these species are rare and expensive, but, when an aquarium is plagued with algae, they are certainly worth the outlay.

The *Hypostomus* in the picture can grow to a large size, sometimes more than 8 inches. The *Otocynclus* is more pleasant, but it does not eat quite so much algae.

CHANDA ranga Glass Fish   Plate 91

This beautiful translucent fish formerly caused a great deal of trouble because it fell an easy victim to *ichthyophthiriasis* (popularly known as "ick") and fungi like *Saprolegnia* soon bothered it. Breeding succeeded only sporadically and then in small numbers. The difficulty is not the water, which may be hard and even brackish in native conditions. This typical little carnivorous fish, which does not hurt any others in the tank, probably lacks the correct food which is so essential. It does not seem to favour daphnia, and red mosquito larvae may be too large for it to manage. Small water insects are favourites as are also the ordinary black mosquito larvae. It likes plenty of sun, many plants and algae, so long as they are not the blue-green ones.

This fish is a beautiful little creature, especially when the sun glints on its prismatic colours, mostly brilliant blues, with green and yellow reflections. These colours can never be seen properly in artificial light. For breeding purposes it is necessary to feed the fry immediately with very young so-called *Nauplius* larvae of the Cyclops.

DERMOGENYS pusillus Half Beak   Plate 92

These are ideal little fishes to keep with the Glass Fishes in one tank, They need sunlight and algae and will eat all manner of water insects, even those that live on top of the water. They are adequately equipped for consuming them with their strangely shaped lower jaw. They also often live, like the Glass Fishes, in brackish water, and they easily contract *Ichthyophthiriasis* if they are not fed with all manner of small insects and infusoria.

Some people find it difficult to keep these fishes alive. Others again say: "I don't do anything special, but they keep on breeding".

This proves that the former must somehow make mistakes, either in the feeding of the fishes or in the composition of the water in the tank, or in both. If the advice given in these pages is followed, these mistakes need not occur. Do not, however, attempt to keep this species with "acid water" fishes. Again, as for the Glass Fishes, the temperature must be fairly high 77°-86°F (25-30°C.).

If we observe carefully the newly-born fry, we shall be astonished at their size, which is about half-an-inch. They eat the same food as the parents, only in slightly smaller amounts. Fruit flies are ideal. Do not give them the red mosquito larvae, because these are ground insects and these fishes never go near the bottom.

TOXOTES jaculator Archer Fish   Plate 93

Its popular name of Archer Fish and the Latin name leave no doubt whatever about the prowess of this species. It can live in the same kind of water as the previous two species, but they should not be kept together in the tank, for the little ones might be devoured. Archer Fishes are definitely insect eaters; they are met with only too seldom on account of breeding difficulties. In few instances have successful breeding results been obtained.

This Archer Fish is well-named. If all things are to its liking, it will put on its act. It will take all manner of food, but it lurks and lies in wait for insects above water. If a nice fat blue-bottle settles on a leaf of a water-plant up to 8

89 *Acanthophthalmus
semicinctus*
Coolie

90 *Hypostomus
plecostomus*

(Plate 93 cont'd)

inches above the level of the water, the fish prepares for action. Before we quite realize what is happening, it will eject or "hurl" a large drop of water right on top of the fly, which thereupon falls into the water and is immediately caught and eaten. This fish even manages to catch insects on the wing, in the same manner. In my own aquarium, Archer Fishes seem to be especially fond of those small creamy white butterflies, so often seen fluttering about on warm sunny days.

When I tried to film all this and lit up the aquarium from above with two large bulbs, one fish spat a drop of water against the hot lamp, which promptly burst.

91 *Chanda ranga*
Glass Fish

92 *Dermogenys pusillus*
Half Beak

93 *Toxotes jaculator*
Archer Fish

PANTODON buchholzi Butterfly Fish   Plate 94

This fish, if well fed, will grow to a considerable size, though not much larger than 5 inches in an aquarium, which for this specimen, should hold about 15 gallons or more. I have not yet heard of successful breeding in these conditions.

The Butterfly Fish does not spit water at the insects above the water level, it just leaps for them. Leaps of 6 feet are quite common. It will not take food under the surface of the water. Maybe it does not see it. Could those enormous pelvic fins be feelers to warn the owners against danger from below? Whatever the case may be, this is an interesting fish which demands a lot of care. It will take small strips of lean raw beef, pieces of meal worm, and such-like, from the fingers if enough patience is exercised.

Some keepers of large aquaria abroad have managed to breed some young which look like tadpoles. The female fish, usually larger than the male, will start to swim underneath him. Then it looks as though he attaches himself to her back with his ventral fins. He slithers down backwards when she halts tremblingly. The eggs are then released while, like many other fishes, the pair huddle closely together, trembling slightly.

RIVULUS cylindraceus   Plate 95

The spreading of certain species over the world is really very wonderful. Salmanders are found only in the northern hemisphere, but each Continent in the southern hemisphere has at least one species of lung fish, which resemble a salamander but is still really and truly a fish.

Africa and South America can boast of many Characins in similar circumstances. Africa and Asia again have similar groups of labyrinth, bubble-fishes etc.

Here we have a few examples of the great group of *Rivulus,* which in shape habit and mode of life largely resemble the vast group of *Aphyosemion* species. The *Rivulus* are Americans and the *Epiplatys* and *Aphyosemion* are Africans. The *Aplocheilus* are found in Asia. These are, as a rule, a little more ferocious, but, in the main, clearly the counterpart of the *Rivulus*. All these types live in shallow waters, which are liable to dry up in hot weather. One, however, is more adequately equipped for this eventuality than the others, namely the *Cynolebias*. We shall discuss these groups and their adaptability.

RIVULUS ocellatus   Plate 96

Rivulus ocellatus is most often met with in the aquaria of the fanciers; but in fact it is the least beautiful of its kind. It can, however, stand the cold, does not sicken quickly, and is easily bred. The difference in sex is sufficiently evident for an amateur to determine; the black eye-like spot at the root of the tail is not found on the adult males.

The fairly large eggs are deposited near the bottom, preferably between plants and they usually remain stuck there. The hatching is very peculiar; some emerge after a week, while others only hatch out after six weeks. The fry differ greatly in size.

It lays eggs only when the water is very shallow and warm at a temperature of 86°F (30°C).

Those eggs are laid while the parents crawl one behind the other through the maze of plants in the very shallow water. The female leads by a head.

The name "ocellatus" denotes the eye-like spot.

EPIPLATYS dageti Firemouth Epiplatys   Plate 97

Of all the species, this is possibly one of the most popular; it is a true old favourite, which, though sometimes superseded by more fashionable types, still manages to hold its own in a good collection. It is a beautiful fish, especially the male with his typical blood-red under-jaw; we continually see that jaw because it is always on the surface. These fishes are always moving about among the floating green; *Riccia* especially is suitable for them. The eggs, which are fairly large, will stick between the greenery.

Time and again the male will look for the female, or she looks for him. When we watch the pair for a little while, we can see an egg appear suddenly. It is immediately fertilised. Both fishes tremble, though not violently. In this way only one egg is laid at a time and it may take days before the next one appears: that will depend on food and temperature. The eggs hatch after eight to fourteen days. Breeding succeeds best by removing the egg-laden *Riccia* from the tank to a special small breeding tank and replacing it with fresh plants. The small fry can, immediately eat sieved daphnia, but care must be taken to see that the older fry do not devour their newly-hatched brothers and sisters.

APLOCHEILUS lineatus   Plate 98

Some time ago, when this fish and its relations were seen very much more than they are to-day, they were called *Panchax*. I believe this name has now entirely disappeared, except for a species in India, the *Aplocheilus panchax*. It is such a pity that, with the name, the fishes seem to have disappeared as well. On the other hand this should cause little surprise, for, though they are certainly beautiful, they will devour smaller fishes.

Should you have the opportunity, try and keep some and study them carefully. They are grateful fish, and will soon take titbits from the fingers such as small pieces of raw meat. Their whole build reveals them as marauders.

94 *Pantodon buchholzi*
Butterfly Fish

95 *Rivulus cylindraceus*

96 *Rivulus ocellatus*

97 *Epiplatys dageti*
Firemouth Epiplatys

One of the few Epiplatys species that will live in friendly relationships with other fish in a community tank.

(Plate 98 cont'd)

Observe the coloured edge along the tail. With some fishes this is coloured red, some yellow, and others green or blue. I have even seen some red above and green below and vice versa.

More eggs are deposited at one time than in the case of the *Epiplatys dageti*. The hatching takes longer; from ten days to a month and even more. Young which hatch last of all develop slowly and mature only after two years.

98 *Aplocheilus lineatus*

93

APHYOSEMION

This generic name means "the little fish with a flag" and was inspired by the handsome fins of the males.

These are egg-laying fishes of tropical West Africa, where they inhabit small bodies of water—ponds, streams, ditches and backwaters, well provided with floating or rooted vegetation. Some of these waters are temporary and disappear as the dry season progresses. The species best adapted to such conditions lay their eggs in the soft bottom debris or mud, where they can survive a long drought. During the dry period, development of the embryo is halted and hatching, followed by further development, takes place only when the rains come again.

In *Aphyosemion,* such an adaption is only achieved in a few species, and in those it is less complete than in the related *Nothobranchius,* or in their South American cousin *Cynolebias.*

Other species of *Aphyosemion* lay their eggs on water-plants, to which they adhere by means of microscopic threads on the egg shell.

The naming of *Aphyosemion* species has proved difficult because the most reliable distinguishing features are the colour-patterns and all but the black parts of these have disappeared when the dead, preserved fish reaches the museum zoologist. For this reason mistakes have been made in the past, and aquarists must be prepared to change the names of some of their favourites as more knowledge of the living fishes in their natural homes comes to light.

Another cause of confusion is the dulness and uniformity of the females of related species of *Aphyosemion,* in contrast to the bright and distinctive colours of the males. One of these modestly coloured females sent from Liberia to the German aquarist, J. Arnold, in 1908 was named for him by the British Museum zoologist Boulenger (*Aphyosemion*) *liberiense*. After this no one in Europe, on receiving a male *Aphyosemion* from West Africa, could be sure that it was or was not the male of *A. liberiense,* so they were all given new names. Recently the Danish zoologist, H. Sfenholt Clausen, went to Liberia to see for himself and his conclusion has been published in the magazine *Ichthyologica*. The only female fish in the neighbourhood of Monrovia corresponding to *Aphyosemion liberiense* was swimming with males that had been named *calabaricus* by Ahl in 1936. This handsome species must now go by the earlier name given to the female, and the *A. calabaricum* of the aquarists must be known as *A. liberiense*. Such changes are a bother, but they are the price we must pay for increased knowledge and the rectification of mistakes of the past.

APHYOSEMION caeruleum Blue Gularis   Plate 99

This beautiful species lives in the Niger Delta and the Cameroons; it lays its eggs on the bottom.

APHYOSEMION bivittatum   Plate 100

Another species of the Cameroons and southern Nigeria. Its eggs adhere to the plants.

APHYOSEMION calliurum   Plate 101

A species of the swampy waters of southern Nigeria, it is equally satisfied to lay its eggs on plants or on the bottom, and the embryo is able to survive within the egg in damp surroundings for a couple of months.

APHYOSEMION sjoestedti Sierra Leone Aphyosemion   Plate 102

The name *sjoestedti* was first given to a species living in the Cameroons and does not really belong to the species of Plate 102, a native of Sierra Leone. We use it here because it is so used in all the aquarium books; and this fish would otherwise be left without a name. If you have a pair, it would be best to call them by their English name for the time being and watch the aquarium journals for the change.

This is one of the species best adapted for drought. It is a bottom-spawner and the development within the egg may be held up for months during the dry season. When these fishes have deposited their eggs, the parents should be removed and a few drops of disinfectant, like formalin, added to the contents of the tank. The water must be drained away very slowly, so that the bottom is no longer covered by it. Then leave everything for a month or two, at the end of which time water to which some rotting hay has been added should be poured into the tank, and after a few days the young fry will appear.

The benefit of the addition of rotting vegetable matter has been discovered empirically by fish-breeders, and it has been suggested that the bacteria concerned in the rotting process help hatching by breaking down the egg shell.

99 *Aphyosemion*
   caeruleum
   Blue Gularis

100 *Aphyosemion*
    bivittatum

101 *Aphyosemion*
    calliurum

102 *Aphyosemion sjoestedti*
Sierra Leone
Aphyosemion

103 *Aphyosemion gulare*
Yellow Gularis

APHYOSEMION gulare Yellow Gularis   Plate 103

This species was first collected in the Niger delta and was so named because of the red colour of its throat, or gular region. Its colours are variable and our picture does not show two blue bands which usually streak the body from head to tail. The ground colour of the dorsal and anal fins and the middle part of the caudal are usually yellow. The males fight together, so it is inadvisable to keep more than one pair in a tank. The eggs are laid on the bottom.

APHYOSEMION multicolor   Plate 104

Although the colours are characteristic for each species, some allowance must be made for variation. It now seems likely that Herr Meinken, the experienced aquarist who named this species, was really dealing with a variety of *Aphyosemion bivittatum* and the name *multicolor* is redundant. Our two pictures (plates 100 and 104) will give an idea of the variation to be expected in *A. bivittatum*.

I am sorry to give the reader an impression of chaos in the group *Aphyosemion,* but some able people are now tackling the problems both in Africa and in their aquaria, and in a few years not only should we be able to name our species correctly, but we should know something about the way of life of most of them, and from that should learn how to keep and breed them in the aquarium.

CYNOLEBIAS belottii Argentine Pearl Fish   Plate 105

The adjustments in climatic conditions which I have described for the *Aphyosemion* have been brought almost to perfection by the beautiful Argentine Pearl Fish.

The country of origin, Argentine, has a sub-tropical steppe with a very hot dry period and a rainy season with greatly varying temperatures. These fishes, therefore, can be kept in our climes without extra heating. But even with the best possible care, they do not survive. A life span of ten months is normal. Then they languish and, except in a very few instances, die within the year. From the age of three months onwards, however, they have laid eggs in mud-holes on the bottom of the tank. In their natural surroundings this laying of eggs begins after the cold wet period, when the pools start to dry out and become hot. The pools eventually dry up entirely, but by that time the parents have died a natural death.

The mud remains slightly humid and this is enough to keep the eggs alive. It has even been proved that young developing from such eggs are stronger than those which do not experience drought. When the rains come, the pools formed are immediately populated by fishes!

CALLICHTHYS callichthys Armoured Catfish   Plate 106

Quite a different adaptation to the drying-out of their pools and puddles is shown by these Armoured Catfishes, which in other ways are most primitive. As mentioned in Plate 89 illustrating the Coolie, this species has an intestinal breathing apparatus. The Coolies die fairly soon when they are out of water. Their intestinal breathing functions only when the water has a low oxygen content. In the case of the Armoured Catfish, the intestines breathe instead of the gills, when the water runs away. The principle seems rather similar to that of the Climbing Fish or Skipper of the Indian Archipelago which I covered in Part One. These Catfish (which may grow a little too large for the average aquaria) dig themselves in during the dry season, just as do the lung fishes. If you happen to be standing by a dry river bed, you can hear a continuous grunting by day, caused by the escaping gases (breathing gases) coming from the intestines of these fishes. It is practically impossible to hear them at night owing to the croaking of frogs.

These fishes are not quiet, neither are they obviously beautiful, but whoever seriously searches for beauty will nevertheless find it here.

APISTOGRAMMA ramirezi   Plate 107

APISTOGRAMMA agassizi Yellow Dwarf Cichlid   Plate 108

These Dwarf Cichlids have not been long kept by amateurs. Sometimes they will do very well in a community tank. It is essential that the water be soft and alkaline and also that rocks and holes are available.

There are, of course, more species than the two illustrated. However, I personally like these best of all and when a few couples are kept in an aquarium there are wonderful skirmishes between the imposing looking males. If the aquarium is large enough, every male makes out his own territory which is defended by skirmishes. I never saw any real damage done, provided that the tank was large enough. Nor did I notice any damage with the *agassizi* but at first sight one would expect the worst with them going for each other like game-cocks. The females modestly swim in between, until they are ripe. This is indicated in the case of the *ramirezi* by a beautiful red on the side and in the case of the *agassizi* by the merging yellow on the brown-yellow colouring.

When the females are ready to spawn they challenge the males to chase them.

On the top of, or underneath, a smooth stone or a strong leaf, the eggs are deposited which will be fertilised by the male.

104 *Aphyosemion multicolor*

105 *Cynolebias bellottii*
Argentine Pearl Fish

106 *Callichthys callichthys*
Armoured Catfish

107 *Apistogramma ramirezi*

108 *Apistogramma agassizi*
Yellow Dwarf Cichlid

109 *Cichlasoma severum*

The female *agassizi* is entirely "boss" in the home. This is also the case with the *ramirezi,* where the difference in size is less striking.

It is only when "he" behaves exactly as "she" wishes that the union seems to be harmonious. But if "he" has the audacity not to conform, then "she" will attack him furiously and bite viciously. This big, good-natured male will then take himself off and will wait until she needs him again for a subsequent nest.

The eggs will usually come to nothing in a community tank, but that does not matter so much. It is wonderful to see how the female feels along the eggs with her mouth, and fans them. Then, when the young appear, they are guarded by the mother and, if "he" is still there, by the father also. In a large well-planted aquarium possibly one youngster will reach maturity. If we seriously intend to breed, the other fishes must be removed, but it is not advisable to remove the *Apistogrammas* for they seem to become attached to their own habitual surroundings.

CICHLASOMA severum   Plate 109

Plates 107 and 108 have introduced the Cichlids, but the enthusiast should try some of the larger species as well. The Angel Fish is one of them and the *Simphysodom discus* (Plate 114) is another.

Cichlasoma severum lives in Brazil, together with the Angel Fish and many other Cichlids. Moreover, these fishes have much more personality than have the little Characins and Barbs. The latter are nearly always "shoal" fishes and react with no rhyme or reason.

The Cichlids live when mature a very lonely existence, at least for the greater part of the year. By "lonely" I mean not together in shoals, but as a pair, male and a female. Therefore, every individual fish has to watch for an enemy marauder; it must take much more notice of its surroundings than when it was in a group or shoal. It consequently learns more. Experience has shown me that they get to know their keeper well and react to him personally; they also learn to receive their food in a certain way. Not that they are at all clever; on the contrary, one is often astonished at their crass stupidity.

AEQUIDENS pulcher Blue Acara   Plate 110

The fish shown in this plate become fairly large; both sexes may grow to 8 inches, although they seldom attain that length in our aquaria. A sizable aquarium of 3 feet 6 inches by 20 inches wide and deep is, however, a necessity, with a flooring of well-washed gravel sand and some smooth stones. We should also do well to give the fishes rocks at the back and sides of the tank. A single *Vallisneria gigantea* might be planted here and there, and set in small flower pots, the draining holes of which have been slightly enlarged. The flower pot must be upside down so that the plant can grow through the hole, and heavy stones piled round it. We can set *Cabomba* in the same way, as we see in the background picture of Plate 111. Most of the Cichlids are real diggers and burrowers and would destroy every plant not safeguarded in this way.

The *Cabomba* is sometimes hard put to it to survive and therefore the better choice may be the Giant Vallisneris. The Amazon Sword Plant also lends itself extraordinarily well to such an aquarium.

HEMICHROMIS bimaculatus Jewel Fish   Plate 111

NANNOCHROMIS nudiceps Blue Cichlid   Plate 112

Just as a diversion I would like to present two Cichlids from Africa. The first is known to be very prone to cannibalism, while the second is quite the contrary. Neither is quite so large as the previous couple, but they are most certainly not Dwarf Cichlids, although the *Nannochromis nudiceps* is more nearly related to that species.

Like the previous two species, these will also dig up plants and even eat them. Strangely enough, this again is quite an individual matter for now and again we find specimens which do not behave in this way. I have never yet owned or cared for a *Nannochromis nudiceps,* so I cannot write from experience, but for breeding purposes it is similar to Dwarf Cichlids.

These fishes are strong and the only thing we really have to be particular about is to siphon away any dirt which may lie on the bottom, so that the well-washed flooring is not soiled by the excreta of the fish nor by decomposing parts of plants.

Time and again these fishes are seen biting into the sandy bottom and then come swimming to the top, munching away all the time and spitting out. I have noticed this especially if there is something to their liking which they have been accustomed to find on the bottom, but they cease these little games if they find nothing. If they are fed red mosquito larvae, which immediately dig themselves into the bottom, then they come to expect that something may always be found there.

Readers should also examine the large picture of *Cichlasoma meeki* (Plate 121). We see in these wonderful pictures of Mr. Rein Stuurman exceptional beauty, colour and shape.

110 *Aequidens*
  pulcher
  Blue Acara

111 *Hemichromis*
  bimaculatus
  Jewel Fish

112 *Nannochromis*
  nudiceps
  Blue Cichlid

113 *Cichlasoma facetum*
Chanchito

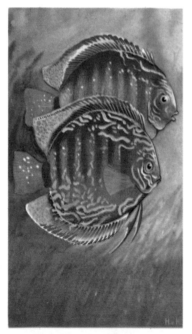

114 *Symphysodon discus*

115 *Monocirrhus polyacanthus*
Leaf Fish

CICHLASOMA facetum Chanchito   Plate 113

SYMPHYSODON discus Discus or Pompadour Fish   Plate 114

All Cichlids should be kept at a fairly high temperature, not below 76°F (24°C). It is only during the winter that the temperature may fall to 70°F (21°C). As soon as a little more warmth is supplied in the Spring, the mating season begins, and with it comes the definition of the boundaries of personal territory. Every male with any self-respect tries to become Lord of the Manor, or rather of his part of the tank. He will chase away every fish, as well as fe- males of his own species. Soon there will be one female who will not allow herself to be chased away, and she becomes his lady. They then together defend their domain, and will chase away every other fish that dares to put in a fin.

The husband and wife vigorously clean some leaves (which should be provided for them), and when this is done to their satisfaction the female passes her genital opening, which has then become prominent, along a leaf from bottom to top, laying a row of adherent eggs, followed by other parallel rows. The male passes over them in the same order, fertilizing as he goes.

When the eggs begin to hatch the young are sucked out of the shells by the parents and spat on to another leaf, to which they adhere by little threads of a sticky substance produced from their heads. After about three days hanging so, the young become free-swimming.

They can then be seen gliding over the body, first of one parent, then the other, evidently feeding on the slime which at this time is secreted in abundance by the skin of the parents. At night the brood hang on the under side of a leaf and the parents stay near them. In the morning the young start feeding again from the parents' skin, the parents alternately providing food and guarding. Gradually the young supplement this babyfood with small organisms from the water. The aquarist should be ready to provide rotifers, *Daphnia* and minute worms.

By this time the young have lost the glands which produce the adhesive substance, and no longer hang on a leaf. They remain at night in a little swarm near the parents. But even when they are 5/8 of an inch long and are able to feed themselves they still pick at the parents' skin occasionally. When they are about an inch long they are weaned.

This discovery was made and published in June 1956 simultaneously by Mr. & Mrs. Roy Skipper in England and Dr. E. Schmidt in Frankfurt-am-Main.

All cichlids care for their young in some way, but the Discus is the only one known to provide special baby-food. Some of the others cradle the eggs and young in the mouth (e.g. *Hemihaplochromis multicolor*, p. 43).

MONOCIRRHUS polyacanthus Leaf Fish   Plate 115

This fish is a very rarely included in an aquarium for it is a voracious eater of small fishes. It has a peculiar way of catching its prey. It stands almost still —not like a pike, completely immobile, but with the slightest movement of breast and dorsal fins. It often postures, as shown here, standing on its head, not really still but gently falling like a leaf. Then again, it will lie almost on its side; in that case the head is the highest point, but it watches for prey all the time. It does not make a dart for it, but moves towards it in a whirling action. Then suddenly its mouth shoots forward like a great trumpet, such as you never see in any other fish, and the prey has disappeared before it has realised its danger. The actions of the Leaf Fish are in keeping with its name.

I have never read or heard of breeding with this fish, but I should imagine it would not be too difficult. It is related to the *Badis badis* (Plate 48) and also to the *Polycentrus schomburgki* which has been bred in captivity.

ELECTROPHORUS electricus   Plate 116

This is an extraordinarily interesting fish, but one which I certainly cannot advise anyone to purchase for a very good reason. It can give real, electric shocks, which can paralyse the arm touching the fish and are most unpleasant.

In other ways too, these fishes are really only suitable for large public aquaria. They can grow to a considerable size, more than three feet long, and as thick as a man's arm. They are certainly not beautiful at that stage, neither are they pleasant in behaviour. To tell the truth I have never seen them as beautiful as they look in the accompanying picture, and only very rarely has any literature about them mentioned the orange colouring they are said to have underneath at a very early age.

Smaller fishes cannot be kept in the same tank; they would be eaten immediately. There are other species of fishes which are able to give electric shocks, for example the Electric Ray found in the Mediterranean. Those shocks seem only to be applied in case of defence. Time and again one hears the story that the natives send large domestic animals into the pools where these fishes live. Those large mammals are better able to withstand the shocks, and the electricity in the fishes is discharged. Then the natives move in and catch the fish.

PHALLOCEROS caudimaculatus   Plate 117

I cannot understand why this species is so seldom seen. During the 1920's it was often met with and called *"Girardinus januarius"*. Later it was proved not to be a *Girardinus,* but, on account of the large horn on the gonopodium of the male, it was given the name of *Phalloceros*. It is very easy-going and does not

116 *Electrophorus*
electricus

117 *Phallocerus*
caudimaculatus

118 *Monodactylus*
argenteus

119 *Brachygobius nunus*
Goby

even require warmth, except at breeding-time, when the temperature must be raised to 86°F (30°C). During the winter no harm is done even if ice should form in the tank. Therefore, it is also an ideal little fish for the garden pond, though it should be taken indoors if serious frost be threatened.

In Argentina it is usually met without the black spots, but in our aquaria we seldom meet it plain.

MONODACTYLUS argenteus   Plate 118

This fish which also possesses the now discarded name of *Psettus argenteus* is not very well known. It is beautiful but nothing like so gaudy as others of the marine species. It is a typical brackish-water fish, but is found in the sea.

It is so adaptable that it can be kept in fresh water. The preliminaries for mating have been observed in an ordinary aquarium, but personally I have never yet heard or read about breeding actually being successful. We depend entirely on imports of this species and that is one of the reasons why it is so rarely seen. I believe that it should be possible to breed it in an aquarium. It is a near relative of the *Monodactylus sebae,* which I have never yet seen in Europe. It comes from the Congo and breeds in fresh water, but as a mature fish often migrates to the river mouth. It resembles a cross between an *argenteus* and an Angel Fish.

120 *Scatophagus argus*
Spotted Scat

BRACHYGOBIUS nunus Goby   Plate 119

Like the *Monodactylus* species, the Goby is a fish of the seashore. It must be able to stand fresh water, for, after torrential rains, it is more than possible that the pool in which it lives is left suddenly with very little salt content. It is also quite possible to keep the groundings or loaches of our own coast in fresh water. They will withstand high temperatures, as well as sudden low ones, quite well. The shallow rocky pools are sometimes much warmer than the sea water quite near, as presumably we have all experienced when paddling. When the tide comes in all the cold sea water comes rushing in to fill the pools; though the water becomes much colder these little fishes just take it all in their stride.

The *Brachygobius* shown here is no exception to this rule. The breeding is fairly successful in fresh water aquaria. Yet we see this variety very rarely, and then mainly as an import from India. Most people like these little beauties, so that cannot be the reason for their scarcety. I have never heard of a third generation having been bred in an aquarium, which raises the point that it may be necessary for their constitution to have sea water from time to time as they do in their natural conditions.

SCATOPHAGUS argus Spotted Scat   Plate 120

The last of the fishes in this book is the Spotted Scat. Two species are regularly met with: one has black spots on an olive green ground and the other has beautiful brilliant red on its back. The latter is so striking in appearance that it attracts everyone. However, it cannot go into a tank together with the Characins; it would eat them first and later die. Characins must have an acid aquarium, and these fishes from the river mouths cannot possibly stand that. Salt or fresh water is all the same to them, but most definitely NOT acid.

The shape of the last three species, and most especially the last one, gives an idea of the marine fish. The Spotted Scat even creates the illusion of a coral fish. It can become quite a pet, watching for its master. Anyone who starts thinking about a marine household aquarium, could well begin with these last three. The salt percentage need not be as high as for real coral fish, nor need the temperature be so constant. These fishes are more resistant to high temperatures than those along our sea shores.

PART THREE

THE KEEPING OF AN AQUARIUM
THE HEALTH OF FISHES

Notes contributed by
THE BRITISH AQUARISTS STUDY SOCIETY

121 *Cichlasoma meeki*

The keeping of an aquarium

In introducing the English edition of this book, we feel that there are certain notes relating to the experiences of aquarists in the British Isles which would be helpful. We are therefore adding them for the benefit of the reader who, having read this book, finds his interest sufficiently aroused to try and keep a few fishes for himself, and would like the additional information.

We are not in this small compass trying to set out a comprehensive treatise on fish-keeping and the finest advice we can offer the novice is to try and join an aquarist society in his own district, or to seek the advice of an established local aquarist. A little personal assistance from the knowledgeable is worth all the books in the world to the would-be keeper of fishes.

TANK SIZE

A number of logical questions will immediately spring to mind. For instance, what size tank and where to keep it? What other requirements are there?

The first tank should not be too small, not so much because of the limitation on the number of fishes it will hold, though this will surely be a stumbling block as soon as the real interest grows, but it has been proved that very small tanks are much more difficult to manage. We would suggest that a start is made with a standard 24 inches × 12 inches × 12 inches tank; a 24 inches × 15 inches × 12 inches tank is rather more attractive because of its greater depth but it will not house any more fishes than the other tank. The limiting factor is the superficial area of the water and NOT the capacity of the tank.

When deciding where to site your tank once it has been obtained, several factors should be borne in mind. It must be near an electrical point, it must be reasonably accessible for feeding and cleaning purposes, and it must be on a substantial base. Water weighs 10 lbs per gallon and a tank of the size that we suggest will weigh over 1 cwt. when filled with water, compost and rocks. You may be tempted to site it in a window; remember that the excessive amount of light that it will receive in such a location may give rise to the growth of microscopic algae which will very rapidly make the water like 'pea soup'.

LIGHTING AND HEATING
Whilst natural light has certain advantages, artificial light is very much easier to control and a situation that has little or no natural light can well be used with the aid of electric light bulbs held in a suitable reflector close to the surface of the water. Furthermore, the British climate being what it is, it will be necessary to provide heating for the tank and a draughty situation in a window can add appreciable to the cost of heating.

The method we recommend from experience is an electric immersion heater, very reliable types of which can be purchased from dealers in aquarium appliances at reasonable prices; we suggest that for the tank size mentioned a heater rated at 100 watts is ample. You will also require a thermostat to control the heater and we suggest that an external type be used as this is very much easier to adjust. A thermometer will also be necessary to measure the temperature of the water and so enable the thermostat to be adjusted correctly and also to check its operation afterwards from time to time.

GRAVEL AND ROCK
To complete our first requirements we shall also want some gravel, or compost as it is called, and plants. We would suggest one or two pieces of rock which when skilfully used can greatly enhance the artistic appearance of our finished aquarium.

Having obtained our tank and other necessities and decided where it is to go, we can now proceed. First, tank must be well washed and rinsed, care being taken to see that every last trace of soap or other cleansing agent used is quite washed away. Next the compost must be well washed; this is best accomplished a little at a time in a bucket under a running tap. The washing should continue until all the cloudiness has vanished when the compost is stirred up. Having stood the tank in position (it must on no account ever be moved when filled with water), the compost can now be put in. It should be about 2 inches to 3 inches deep at the back sloping down to about 1 inch at the front. This is done to assist in the cleaning of the tank afterwards when the fish are living in it. The rock can now be placed in position. A word on the selection of this. Only hard weathered rock should be used and limestone and marble are quite unsuitable. Sharp edges and splinters on which the fish might injure themselves must be removed. It will be found easier to place plants in the tank if it contains two or three inches of water and this can now be added, care being taken not to stir up the compost in the process. This can be done by pouring the water on to a saucer placed on top of the gravel.

WATER
Ordinary tap water is quite suitable for the majority of tropical fishes and the beginner is strongly advised to avoid species whose water requirements are more selective until more experience has been gained.

PLANTS
The plants may now be introduced. Rooted species should be planted like ordinary terrestrial plants but care should be taken not to cover the crowns, that is where the stalks ascend from the roots. Cuttings and plants without roots may be held down by tying to a small pebble with fine thread or weighted down with some fine strip lead. The plants are best concentrated at the back and sides of the tank, particularly in the rear corners. The object is to try and create an illusion of space and an artistic

effect at the same time allowing the fishes to be seen to their best advantage.

Once planting is completed, the tank may be filled with water. The best way to accomplish this without too much disturbance is to lay a sheet of newspaper so as to completely cover the surface and then pour the water on to this from a jug or better still a watering can with a rose fitting so that the water is broken up into a fine spray. When the tank is full the newspaper can be removed.

ELECTRICAL CIRCUIT

At this stage the heater and thermostat may be introduced. These should be spaced well apart, preferably at opposite ends of the tank. The necessary connections of wiring should be made according to the makers' instructions, but NO CONNECTIONS TO THE SUPPLY until everything is in place and has been checked. The heater should be arranged at the rear of the tank concealed possibly be a rock or the plants but so that the water can circulate freely round it. The thermostat fixed into position at the opposite end and when all is secure—and not before—the current may be turned on. The thermometer should be placed in the tank and the whole installation left for several hours to allow time for the heater to warm the water. Several readings of the thermometer should then be noted at intervals of an hour or so and if necessary the thermostat adjusted so that the average temperature is about 72° F. (22° C.). A variation of a few degrees either way should be looked for and it will be found that your fishes are healthier and hardier than if they are kept at a constant and unvarying temperature.

FISHES

The aquarium should now be left to settle down for a few days. Resist the temptation to put fishes in straight away and wait just that few days to give the plants time to become established and the water time to settle down.

116

Start off with fishes that are hardy and not too fussy about their requirements, probably the best and most easily obtainable for this purpose in this country are the Guppy and the Platy. When you have read this book you will probably have some idea of what you want to keep, but for a start and to gain experience you cannot better the two we have mentioned.

If you bring your fish home in a jar or polythene bag, do not tip them straight into the tank but float the container with the fishes in on the surface of the tank until the temperatures are within a degree of each other, then gently lower the jar or bag into the water and allow your fishes to swim out.

DRY FEEDING

For a staple diet use a good proprietory dried food of which there are a number on the market. Do not choose one kind and stick to it but obtain two or three and give your fishes a variety. Great attention must be paid to the matter of feeding. It has been said many times and with great truth that more fishes are killed by overfeeding than by underfeeding. Strictly speaking fishes do not overfeed but the food that they do not consume rapidly decomposes and pollutes the water with very serious consequences. Only experience can dictate how much to feed, but feed sparingly at first, not more than one feed a day. Watch your fishes feed and try to feed just the amount that is completely eaten up in ten minutes, no more. When you have gained some experience you can increase the number of feeds to 3 or 4 times a day but be absolutely sure that all the food is consumed on each occasion.

LIVE FEEDING

In addition to dried foods, live foods may be given, if and when obtainable. Daphnia and tubifex are sometimes obtainable from pet shops and dealers and sometimes mosquito larvae can be collected; all these are excellent foods and will add to the well-being of your fishes. Chopped meat, chopped earthworm and even cheese may be given as an occasional treat but great care must be taken to see that none is left over to decompose on the tank bottom.

CLEANING

When your tank has been installed for a few weeks it will be noticed that a certain amount of dirt or 'mulm' has accumulated on the bottom of the tank. This is not harmful but rather unsightly so syphon it off with a piece of rubber tubing, replace the water so removed with fresh water of approximately the same temperature. Never completely change the water except as an emergency measure to deal with severe contamination. This should never occur and is a sign of mismanagement. Do not change the water if it turns green. Just leave it to clear naturally but reduce the amount of light to prevent repetition of this phenomenon. You may deal with this mulm by running a filter, operated by a small electric pump and this will keep your tank clean, but this is by no means essential.

In addition to the items mentioned already, you will need a net to catch your fishes if and when required, a scraper to remove the algal growth from the front glass of the tank from time to time and you may find a pair of planting sticks a useful accessory to deal with any of the plants that become disturbed or uprooted during the course of operations on the tank.

The health of fishes

The would-be aquarist who reads a treatise on fish diseases is apt to become despondent and think that the keeping and rearing of healthy fishes may be beyond his capabilities. Nothing could be further from the truth as fishes kept in good conditions are remarkably resistant to disease. Indeed, while the known diseases are legion, only a few can be said commonly to occur.

It should be understood that diseases are only introduced into an aquarium and provided that one starts with a healthy stock and reasonable precautions are taken, no trouble should be experienced.

Fish diseases and parasites should not occur in water where no fish are present and therefore the introduction of live foods such as daphnia and mosquito larvae are usually fairly safe. This is because these creatures are only to be collected in usable numbers in waters that do not contain living fishes. More care must be taken however in the feeding of tubifex worms. These are collected from mud banks often situated in sewage outfalls and therefore require cleaning before they are suitable for use as food. Some cleaning is usually done by the shops, but a further washing in a dish of water under a gently running tap for a few hours is a wise precaution. Some aquarists will not feed tubifex to fishes unless it has been treated in some form of sterilising fluid in case it is carrying some form of disease. Half an hour's immersion in a few drops of Malachite Green Solution in the water of the dish in which the worms are lying should stop any trouble of this kind, but this must be followed by a further wash in clear water for half an hour to clear the dye from the worms before they are fed.

Live foods from terrestrial sources such as whiteworm *(Enchytrae)* and earthworms should be quite safe.

Fish and plants may however be carrying disease or parasites and it is good practice to isolate or quarantine all new arrivals. This simply means putting them in a separate tank or container for about two weeks. If the fish appear to be quite healthy at the end of this time, they can be transferred to their new home.

HEALTHY FISH

To be able to judge whether or not a fish is in the best of health is largely a matter of experience. Nevertheless there are certain signs which are good indicators of the healthy state.

The colours of a healthy fish will be bright and clear under normal conditions. A fish will often loose its colour temporarily due to fright and other causes, but persistent fading of colour should be regarded with suspicion.

The skin and scales should be free from grey slimy patches or spots (other than normal colouration). Its fins should be free moving and not continually folded. In particular the dorsal fin should be carried erect and very often the drooping of this fin may be the first sign that a fish is 'off colour'.

Gills are normally bright PINK in colour except in some species where they are more deeply pigmented. Pale or even very red gills may be a sign of poor health or parasites.

A flat belly and other signs of wasting are an indication of disease and continually abnormal swelling of the body should be treated with suspicion. The latter, of course, may also indicate that the fish is carrying eggs or fry, a normal and encouraging state of affairs. In the disease known as Dropsy the body is swollen, but the scales also protude from the body giving a feathery appearance.

The healthy fish swims in a normal manner according to the habit of its species. In some species this may mean swimming very near to the surface. In others swimming in the bottom layer of water is the normal habit. Most species swim in the middle layers, but all fishes will swim out of their normal area from time to time.

Some fish are lively swimmers and always in evidence. Others will hide away and appear timid. This is quite normal in some species, but any persistent change in habit may be due to poor health.

Earlier we said that the judging of a fish's health was largely a matter of experience. There are so many variations in appearance and habit in the various species that to lay down precise rules might be misleading. Ideally one should compare a suspected fish with a healthy fish of the same species.

To sum up, fishes kept under good conditions, i.e. adequate but not excessive feeding with the right foods, correct temperature range and hot overcrowded, should remain healthy and not become diseased. Disease can only be introduced, so, if possible, quarantine new arrivals.

SOME FISH DISEASES AND THEIR TREATMENT

White Spot *(Ichthyophthiriasis)*
The most commonly seen aquarium disease takes the form of pin head size white spots on the body and fins of the fish. This is known to the aquarist as White Spot which is very much easier to remember than the scientific name given above. Each of these little white spots is actually a small bubble attached to the body of the fish and contains parasites. These are protozoans with the rather frightening name of *Ichthyophthirias multi-filaris*. While the parasites are still within the thin skin of the bubble they cannot be killed without harming the fish. At one stage of their development however, they leave their host to reproduce by breaking out of the skin and it is at this point they are most vulnerable and can be killed.

There are a number of chemicals and proprietary cures. The

latter should be used in accordance with the manufacturer's instructions. Quinine hydrochloride is an effective treatment although if used in a planted tank it may cause the plants to deteriorate. ½ grain of quinine hydrochloride should be dissolved in each gallon of water and this dose repeated at daily intervals to give a total dose of 1½ grains per gallon. If possible remove the fishes to a separate tank for treatment. If all the fishes are removed from the tank it will be quite safe to use again in two weeks as the parasite will die without a host. It is also advisable to raise the temperature of the water slightly.

The method of treatment that we recommend from experience is the use of medical quality Methylene Blue. 1 c.c. of 1% solution per gallon of water, i.e. if the tank holds 15 gallons then 15 c.c. are needed. Raise the temperature to 80°F (27°C). This speeds up the life cycle of the parasite and hastens the cure which should be effected in 6 or 7 days. This treatment will soften the foliage of the broad leaved plants and may make them very unsightly for a time. To avoid this either treat the fishes in a separate container or preferably remove the plants and replant them when a cure has been effected. This method of treatment will cause none of the side effects that are sometimes associated with other methods of treatment. Do not worry about the colour of the water containing this dye; it will have no effect on the fishes whatsoever.

FUNGUS

Fungus is fairly often seen on fishes. Although this is more common on coldwater fishes, it is sometimes seen in tropical tanks. It is important to remember that fungus does not grow on healthy tissues and that if funges is present, something is wrong! It may be that one fish is attacking the others and in doing so is leaving open wounds for the fungus to take hold. If this is not the case, perhaps a sharp stone or heater is scratching the fishes, or perhaps the fish was damaged by catching it in the net for some reason or another. Whatever the reason try to find it and rectify it before treating the fish.

There are very many types of fungi but all of them appear similar to the amateur aquarist, usually looking like grey or white woolly masses on the fins or body. If the fish is a fairly large one and the areas affected are only few, then the fish can be caught in a large net and the affected parts painted with a weak solution of disinfectant Iodine. (1 part tincture of Iodine with 9 parts of water.) If this does not clear the fungus within a few days then further treatment is necessary. Phenoxetol is the recommended treatment. The infected fish must be treated in a separate tank in a solution of $1\frac{1}{2}$ fluid ounces (3 tablespoonfuls) of 1% Phenoxetol to each gallon of water. The fish may be left in this solution until the cure is complete. This substance is rather difficult to dissolve so care should be taken in the making of the solution.

SWIM BLADDER DISEASE

This is a derangement of the swim bladder which may be due to a variety of causes. Fishes affected have difficulty in maintaining their equilibrium and sometimes swim upside-down or in a vertical position. Given good conditions some fishes recover spontaneously, but usually this condition must be regarded as incurable, although the victims often live for a long time. It is not infectious.

DROPSY

A condition in which fluid accumulates in the tissues causing the body to swell and the scales to stand out from the body giving rise to a feathery appearance. The cause of this disease is not fully understood but it may primarily be due to a virus with bacteria as secondary invaders. At present there is little prospect of success in treating this condition and it is kinder to destroy fish suffering from it. This can be done painlessly by throwing the fish hard on to a concrete floor.

CONCLUSION

A word of caution to the beginner. If your fishes appear unhealthy, do try and get the advice of an experienced aquarist. Do not try and treat a condition unless you are sure of what you are doing. It has been said, with some truth, that more fish die from treatment than from disease. This is probably true because inexperienced aquarists are apt to take out a fish at the first signs of ill health and put it into various chemical solutions which may, or may not, be effective. After all, many fishes recover from diseases by their own natural immunity processes. If you have a spare tank it is always a good idea to isolate a sickly fish, raise the temperature a little and feed it with live food such as daphnia. In this way you will be able to help your fish recover without resorting to more drastic methods. If you need advice your local Aquarist's Society will usually be able to help you. Finally, a word of reassurance, the diseases of fishes CANNOT affect human beings.

The Technical Committee of the British Aquarists Study Society will be pleased to help any person with queries or difficulties with their fishes or aquaria.

We sincerely hope that this book will be the means of introducing you to a fascinating and delightful hobby which will prove a lifelong interest.

LONDON,
February, 1963

The Technical Committee.
British Aquarists Study Society.

INDEX

All references are to pages numbers

Acanthophthalmus semicinctus, ... 86, 88
Acorus pusillus, ... 13, 16, 75
Aequidens pulcher, ... 102-3, 104
Algae, ... 8, 10, 12
Amazon sword plant, ... 53, 54, 103
Ambulia, ... 65
Ameiurus, ... 46
Angel fish, ... 42, 45, 56
Anoptichthys jordani, ... 70, 72
Aphyocharax rubripinnis, ... 46, 48
Aphyosemion bivittatum, ... 95, 96
Aphyosemion caeruleum, ... 95, 96
Aphyosemion calliurum, ... 95, 96
Aphyosemion gulare 97, 98
Aphyosemion multicolor, ... 98, 100
Aphyosemion sjoestedti, ... 95, 97
Apistogramma agassizi, ... 99, 101
Apistogramma ramirezi, ... 99, 101
Aplocheilus lineatus, ... 91, 93
Archer fish, ... 87-8, 89
Argentine pearl fish, ... 98, 100
Armoured catfish, ... 99, 100
Australian rainbow, ... 31, 32

Bacopa caroliniana, ... 20, 21, 66
Badis badis, ... 43, 45
Barb, . 19, 21, 23, 25-31, 32, 79-80, 81-2, 84
Barbus conchonius 19, 21
Barbus fasciatus, ... 30, 32
Barbus gelius, ... 29, 30
Barbus nigrofasciatus, ... 26, 28
Barbus oligolepis, ... 29, 30
Barbus schuberti, ... 27, 29
Barbus semifasciolatus, ... 27, 28
Barbus tetrazona, ... 82, 84
Barbus ticto, ... 19, 26, 28, 30
Barbus titteya 79-80, 81
Beacon fish, ... 50, 52
Belgian flag, ... 66, 67
Belonesox belizanus, ... 15, 17
Betta picta, ... 42, 44
Betta splendens, ... 39, 41, 44
Black belly, ... 66
Black ruby, ... 26, 28
Black sailfin, ... 15
Black tetra, ... 53, 54
Black widow, ... 53, 54
Blind cave fish, ... 70, 72
Bloodfin, ... 46, 48
Blue acara, ... 102-3, 104

Blue cichlid, ... 103, 104
Blue gourami, ... 35, 37
Blue gularis, ... 95, 96
Brachydanio albolineatus, ... 22-3, 24
Brachydanio nigrofasciatus, ... 22, 24
Brachydanio rerio 22, 24
Brachygobius nunus, ... 109, 110
Buenos Aires tetra, ... 49, 50
Butterfly fish, ... 90, 92

Cabomba caroliniana, ... 65-6, 71, 83
Callichthys callichthys, ... 99, 100
Carnegiella strigata, ... 70, 72
Catfish, ... 65-6, 78, 80, 97, 98
Ceratophyllum, ... 9, 18
Ceratopteris thalictroides, . 22, 27, 31-3, 37
Chanchito, ... 105, 106
Chanda ranga,. 86, 89
Characin, ... 46-55, 66-77, 78-9, 110
Chequered barb, ... 29, 30
Chironomid larva 57
Chichlasoma facetum, ... 105, 106
Cichlasoma meeki, ... 61, 103, 112
Cichlasoma severum, ... 101-2
Cichlid, ... 42, 45, 56, 99, 101-6
Clover, ... 80, 82
Colisa fasciata, ... 37
Colisa labiosa, ... 37, 40
Colisa lalia, ... 38, 40
Comet platy, ... 13, 14, 16
Congo characin, ... 75, 77
Coolie, ... 86, 88
Copeina arnoldi, ... 79, 81
Copeina guttata, ... 79, 81
Corynopoma riisei, ... 74, 76
Corydoras arcuatas, ... 78, 80
Corydoras paleatus, ... 46, 48, 78
Croaking gourami, ... 38, 40
Cryptocoryne affinis, ... 66
Cryptocoryne griffithi, ... 66, 68
Cryptocoryne nevelli, ... 66, 68
Ctenobrycon spilurus, ... 71, 73
Cynolebias bellottii, ... 98, 100

Danio, ... 22-3, 24-5
Danio malabaricus, ... 23, 25
Daphnia, ... 6, 57, 117
Dermogenys pusillus, ... 87, 89
Diamond characin, ... 53, 54
Diseases, ... 121-24

Dropsy,....................... 123
Dwarf cichlid,............. 99, 101, 103
Dwarf gourami,................ 38, 40

Echinodorus intermedius, ... 53, 549
Echinodorus radicans, ... 19
Eel grass, ... 17, 22
Egeria densa,............... 10, 11, 12
Egyptian mouth-breeder, ... 43, 45
Electrophorus electricus, ... 107, 108
Eleocharis acicularis, ... 17, 20, 23
Elodea densa, ... 10, 11, 12
Epiplatys dageti,................ 91, 93
Esomus danrica, ...23, 25
Esomus malayensis, ... 25-6

Feather fin, ... 74, 76
Fern,.......................... 32-3
Firemouth Epiplatys, ... 91, 93
Flag fish, ... 46, 48
Flame tetra, ... 46, 47, 49
Flying barb, ... 23-6
Fontinalis, ... 18
Food,.................. 6, 50, 57, 117-8
  see also under names of individual fishes
Four-leaved clover, ... 82, 84
Fourth danio,.................... 22
Fungus,....................... 122-3
Gambusia, ... 10
Giant danio, ... 23, 25
Giant gourami,.................... 37
Girardinus, ... 107
Glass fish, ... 86, 87, 89
Glow light tetra, ... 70-1, 72
Gnat larva. 57
Goby, ... 109, 110
Golden dwarf barb, ... 29, 30
Golden pencil fish, ... 76, 77
Gourami, ... 34-9, 40, 42
"Green" swordtail, ... 14
Guppy, ... 9, 10, 117
Gymnocorymbus ternetzi, ... 53, 54

Hair grass, ... 17, 20, 23
Half beak,..................... 87, 89
Hasemania melanura,............... 50
Hatchet fish, ... 70, 72
Head and tail light fish, ... 50, 51, 52
Heating, ... 114
  see also under names of individual fishes
Helostoma temmincki, ... 34, 36
Hemichromis bimaculatus,...... 103, 104
Hemigrammus caudovittatus, ... 49, 50
Hemigrammus erythrozonus,. 70, 71, 72, 83
Hemigrammus nanus, ... 50, 52

Hemigrammus ocellifer, ... 50, 52
Hemigrammus unilineatus, ... 74, 76
Hemihaplochromis multicolor, ... 43, 45
Heterandria formosa,........... 9, 11, 54
Heteranthera zosteraefolia, . 19, 21, 54, 66
Hockeystick,.................... 73-4
Hornwort,........................ 9
Hydrilla verticillata, ... 83
Hyphessobrycon callistus, ... 67, 69
Hyphessobrycon flammeus, ... 47, 49
Hyphessobrycon gracilis, ... 71
Hyphessobrycon heterorhabdus, ... 68, 69
Hyphessobrycon innesi, ... 70-1, 73
Hyphessobrycon pulchripinnis, ... 66, 68
Hyphessobrycon rosaceus, ... 67, 68
Hypostomus plecostomus, ... 86, 88

Ichthyophiriasis, ... 86, 87, 121-2
Indian fern, ... 31-3
Indian water pest, ... 8-3

Jewel fish, ... 103, 104
Jordanella floridae, ... 46, 48

Kissing gourami, ... 34, 36, 86

Lace gourami, ... 42, 44
Leaf fish, ... 105, 107
Lebistes reticulatis,............... 9, 10
Lemon tetra, ... 66-68, 83
Lighting, ... 114
Limnophila, ... 65, 66
Loach,..................... 84, 86
Loricaria, ... 86
Ludwigia alternefolia, ... 78, 80
Lyre tail, ... 95, 97
Lysimachia,..................... 18

Macropodus opercularis, ... 34, 35, 36
Malayan flying barb, ... 25-6
Marsilea quadrifolia, ... 82, 84
Melanotaenia maccullochi, ... 31, 32
Metynnis roosevelti, ... 47, 49, 71
Midnight mollie, ... 14-15, 17
Minnow, ... 18, 20
Minor, ... 67, 69
Moenkhausia pittieri,............ 53, 54
Moenkhausia sanctaefilomenae, ... 53, 54
Mollienisia velifera, ... 14-15, 16
Moneywort, ... 18
Monocirrhus polyacanthus 105, 107
Monodactylus argenteus, ... 108, 109
Moon platy, ... 13, 16
Mosquito fish, ... 9, 11
Mosquito larvae, ... 10, 26, 75, 84

126

Myriophyllum, ... 18, 20, 27, 71

Naias, ... 18, 47
Nannostomus anomalus, ... 64, 76, 77
Nannochromis nudiceps, ... 103, 104
Neolebias ansorgii, ... 78, 80
Neon tetra, ... 70-1, 73
Nigger barb, ... 26, 28

Otocinclus 86

Pantodon buchholzi, ... 90, 92
Paradise fish, ... 34, 35, 36
Pearl danio, ... 22-3, 24
Pearl leeri, ... 42, 44
Peat, ... 62-3, 78
Pencil fish 75, 76, 77
Penguin fish, ... 73-4
Phailoceros caudimaculatus, ... 107, 108
Phenacogrammus interruptus, ... 45, 46
Plants, 8, 17-18, 19-21, 31-3, 53, 54, 64, 65
66, 68, 80, 82, 84, 115
see also under names of individual fishis
Platy fish, ... 10, 12, 13-14, 16, 117
Platy variatus, ... 15, 17
Poecilobrycon auratus, ... 75, 77, 83
Pristella riddlei, ... 51, 52, 74
Psettus argenteus, ... 109
Pterophyllum scalare 42, 45, 56
Purring gourami, ... 38, 40

Rainbow fish, ... 9, 10
Rasbora heteromorpha, ... 83, 85
Rasbora maculata, ... 83, 85
Rasbora trilineata, ... 82, 85
Red swordtail, ... 12, 13
Riccia, ... 33, 51, 91
Rivulus cylindraceus, ... 90, 92
Rivulus ocellatus, ... 90-1
Rosy barb, ... 19, 21

Sagittaria natans, ... 18, 27
Salvinia auriculata, ... 22, 33
Scatophagus argus, ... 109, 110
Scissors tail, ... 80, 83
Siamese fighting fish, ... 39, 41, 44
Sierra Leone aphyosemion, ... 95, 97
Silver tetra, ... 71, 73
Silver tips, ... 50, 51, 52

Spotted danio, ... 22, 24
Spotted scat, ... 109, 110
Stevardia albipinnis, ... 74
Striped barb, ... 30, 32
Striped gourami, ... 37
Swim bladder disease, ... 123
Sword plant, ... 19
Swordtail, ... 11, 12, 13, 14
Swordtail characin, ... 74, 76
Symphysodon discus, ... 105, 106
Synodontis nigriventris, ... 65

Tanichthys albonubes, ... 18, 20
Tanks, ... 111-12
Tape grass, ... 17, 20
Tetra, ... 49, 50, 53, 54, 66, 68, 70-3
Thayeria sanctaemariae (obliqua), . . . 73-4
Thick-lipped gourami, ... 37, 40
Three spot gourami, ... 35, 36
Tiger barb, ... 82, 83, 84
Tooth carps, ... 10, 15, 16
Toxotes jaculator, ... 87-8, 89
Trichogaster leeri, ... 42, 44
Trichogaster trichopterus, ... 35, 36, 37
Trichopsis vittatus, ... 38, 40
Tubifex, ... 30, 57, 117

Upside down catfish, ... 65-6

Vallisneria gigantea, ... 71
Vallisneria spiralis, ... 17, 20, 23
Velifera mollie, ... 14, 16

Wagtail platy, ... 13-14, 16
Water, ... 61-4, 115
see also under names of individual fishes
Water plants, *see* Plants
White cloud mountain minnow, ... 18, 20
White spot, ... 121-2
Willow moss, ... 18

Xiphophorus helleri, ... 12, 13
Xiphophorus maculatus, . . 10, 12, 13-14, 16
Xiphophorus variatus, ... 15, 17

Yellow dwarf cichlid, ... 99, 101, 102
Yellow gularis, ... 97, 98

Zebra danio, ... 22, 24